Fod[...]

Pocket

Jamaica

Excerpted from *Fodor's Caribbean*

Fodor's Travel Publications, Inc.
New York • Toronto • London • Sydney • Auckland
www.fodors.com

Fodor's Pocket Jamaica

EDITORS: Laura M. Kidder, Christina Knight

Editorial Contributors: Robert Andrews, John Bigley, David Brown, Paris Permenter, Helayne Schiff, M. T. Schwartzman (Essential Information editor)

Editorial Production: Nicole Revere

Maps: David Lindroth, *cartographer;* Steven Amsterdam and Robert Blake, *map editors*

Design: Fabrizio La Rocca, *creative director;* Guido Caroti, *associate art director;* Jolie Novak, *photo editor*

Production/Manufacturing: Mike Costa

Cover Photograph: Piero Ribelli/From the book *Jah Pickney, Children of Jamaica*

Text Design: Between the Covers

Copyright

Special Sales

Fodor's Travel Publications are available at special discounts for bulk purchases for sales promotions or premiums. Special editions, including personalized covers, excerpts of existing guides, and corporate imprints, can be created in large quantities for special needs. For more information, contact your local bookseller or write to Special Markets, Fodor's Travel Publications, 201 East 50th Street, New York, NY 10022. Inquiries from Canada should be directed to your local Canadian bookseller or sent to Random House of Canada, Ltd., Marketing Department, 2775 Matheson Boulevard East, Mississauga, Ontario L4W 4P7. Inquiries from the United Kingdom should be sent to Fodor's Travel Publications, 20 Vauxhall Bridge Road, London SW1V 2SA, England.

PRINTED IN THE UNITED STATES OF AMERICA

10 9 8 7 6 5 4 3 2 1

CONTENTS

Maps

ON THE ROAD WITH FODOR'S

WHEN I PLAN A VA-
CATION, the first
thing I do is cast
around among my friends and col-
leagues to find someone who's
just been where I'm going. That's
because there's no substitute for a
recommendation from a good
friend who knows your tastes,
your budget, and your circum-
stances, someone who's just been
there. Unfortunately, such friends
are few and far between. So it's
nice to know that there's *Fodor's
Pocket Jamaica.*

In the first place, this book won't
stay home when you hit the road.
It will accompany you every step
of the way, steering you away from
wrong turns and wrong choices
and never expecting a thing in return. Most important of all, it's
written and assiduously updated
by the kind of people you *would*
hit up for travel tips if you knew
them. They're as choosy as your
pickiest friend, except they've
probably seen a lot more of Jamaica. In these pages, they don't
send you chasing down every town
and sight on the island but have
instead selected the best sights,
the ones that are worthy of your
time and money.

About Our Writers

Our success in achieving our
goals—and in helping to make
your trip the best of all possible vacations—is a credit to the hard
work of our extraordinary writers.

After honeymooning in Jamaica a
dozen years ago, **Paris Permenter**
and **John Bigley** decided to specialize in writing about and pho-
tographing the Caribbean region.
They're authors of *Caribbean with
Kids, Caribbean for Lovers, Adventure Guide to the Cayman Islands,* and *Adventure Guide to
the Leeward Islands.* Their work
has appeared in publications na-
tionwide. From their home base in
Texas, they've also contributed to
Fodor's *The Southwest's Best Bed
and Breakfasts.*

Connections

We're pleased that the American
Society of Travel Agents contin-
ues to endorse Fodor's as its
guidebook of choice. ASTA is the
world's largest and most influ-
ential travel trade association,
operating in more than 170 countries, with 27,000 members
pledged to adhere to a strict code
of ethics reflecting the Society's

motto, "Integrity in Travel."
ASTA shares Fodor's devotion to
providing smart, honest travel information and advice to travelers,
and we've long recommended
that our readers—even those who
have guidebooks and traveling
friends—consult ASTA member
agents for the experience and pro-
fessionalism they bring to your
vacation planning.

Do check out the World Wide Web
when you're planning. You'll find
everything from up-to-date
weather forecasts to virtual tours
of famous cities. Fodor's Web site,
www.fodors.com, is a great place
to start your on-line travels.

How to Use This Book

Organization

Up front is **Essential Information,**
an easy-to-use section divided al-
phabetically by topic. Under each
listing you'll find tips, addresses,
and phone numbers of organizations and companies that offer
destination-related services and
detailed information and publications.

The first chapter in the guide, Destination: Jamaica, helps get you in
the mood for your trip. Other
chapters cover lodging; dining;
beaches, outdoor activities, and
sports; shopping; nightlife; exploring; and a portrait essay on
spicy jerk cooking.

Icons and Symbols

★   Our special recommenda-
    tions
✕   Restaurant
🏨 Lodging establishment
🐤 Good for kids (rubber
    duckie)
☞   Sends you to another sec-
    tion for more information
✉   Address
☎   Telephone number
☉   Opening and closing times
💰 Admission prices (those we
    give apply to adults; sub-
    stantially reduced fees are
    almost always available for
    children, students, and se-
    nior citizens)

Hotel Facilities

We always list the facilities that are
available—but we don't specify
whether they cost extra: When
pricing accommodations, always
ask what's included. In addition,
assume that all rooms have private
baths unless otherwise noted.

At the end of each review, we list
the meal plans the hotel offers:
All-inclusive (all meals and most
activities), **Breakfast Plan** (BP, with
a full breakfast daily), **Continental Plan** (CP, with a Continental
breakfast daily), **European Plan**
(EP, with no meals), **Full American
Plan** (FAP, with all meals), or **Modified American Plan** (MAP, with
breakfast and dinner daily). The
FAP may be ideal if you're on a
budget, but if you enjoy a differ-

ent dining experience each night, it's better to book rooms on the EP. Since some hotels insist on the MAP, particularly in high season, find out whether you can exchange dinner for lunch or for meals at neighboring hotels.

Caribbean Addresses

"Whimsical" might best describe Caribbean addresses. Streets change name for no apparent reason, maps and signage aren't always reliable, and many buildings have no numbers. We've tried to supply cross streets, landmarks, and other directionals throughout. But to find your destination, you may have to ask a local—and be prepared for such directions as "Take a right at the fish market, then a left where you see the cow pasture."

Restaurant Reservations and Dress Codes

Reservations are always a good idea; we note only when they're essential or when they're not accepted. Book as far ahead as you can, and be sure to reconfirm. Unless otherwise noted, the restaurants listed are open daily for lunch and dinner. We mention dress only when men must wear a jacket or a jacket and tie. Look for an overview in the What to Wear sections of the dining chapter.

Credit Cards

The following abbreviations are used: **AE,** American Express; **D,** Discover; **DC,** Diners Club; **MC,** MasterCard; and **V,** Visa.

Don't Forget to Write

You can use this book in the confidence that all prices and opening times are based on information supplied to us at press time; Fodor's cannot accept responsibility for any errors. Time inevitably brings changes, so always confirm information when it matters—especially if you're making a detour to visit a specific place.

Were the restaurants we recommended as described? Did our hotel picks exceed your expectations? Did you find a museum we recommended a waste of time? Keeping a travel guide fresh and up-to-date is a big job, and we welcome your feedback, positive *and* negative. If you have complaints, we'll look into them and revise our entries when the facts warrant it. If you've discovered a special place that we haven't included, we'll pass the information along to our correspondents and have them check it out. So send us your thoughts via e-mail at editors@fodors.com (specifying the name of the book on the subject line) or on paper in care of the Pocket Jamaica editor at Fodor's, 201 East 50th Street, New York, New York 10022. In the meantime, have a wonderful trip!

Karen Cure
Editorial Director

The Caribbean

THE BAHAMAS

Turks and Caicos Islands

Cuba

Haiti   Hispaniola

Dom Rep

Montego Bay

G R E A T E R

Port-au-Prince

Santo Domin

Kingston

JAMAICA

A N

Caribbean   Sea

Aruba

Willemstad

COLOMBIA   Maracaibo

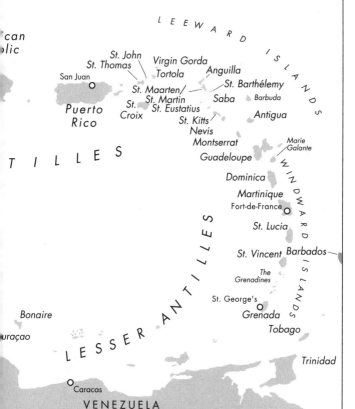

ATLANTIC OCEAN

0 ——— 200 miles
0 ——— 300 km

N

LEEWARD ISLANDS

*can
lic*

San Juan

St. John
St. Thomas

Virgin Gorda
Tortola

Anguilla
St. Barthélemy

*Puerto
Rico*

St.
Croix

St. Maarten/
St. Martin
St. Eustatius

Saba

Barbuda

St. Kitts

Antigua

Nevis

Montserrat

Marie
Galante

Guadeloupe

WINDWARD ISLANDS

T I L L E S

Dominica

Martinique
Fort-de-France

St. Lucia

L E S S E R   A N T I L L E S

St. Vincent   Barbados

The
Grenadines

Bonaire

St. George's

uraçao

Grenada

Tobago

Caracas

Trinidad

VENEZUELA

ESSENTIAL INFORMATION

Basic Information on Traveling in Jamaica, Savvy Tips to Make Your Trip a Breeze, and Companies and Organizations to Contact

AIR TRAVEL

BOOKING YOUR FLIGHT

Price is just one factor to consider when booking a flight: frequency of service and even a carrier's safety record are often just as important. Major airlines offer the greatest number of departures. Smaller airlines—including regional and no-frills airlines—usually have a limited number of flights daily. On the other hand, so-called low-cost airlines usually are cheaper, and their fares impose fewer restrictions, such as advance-purchase requirements. Safety-wise, low-cost carriers as a group have a good history—about equal to that of major carriers.

When you book, **look for nonstop flights** and **remember that "direct" flights stop at least once.** Try to **avoid connecting flights,** which require a change of plane. Two airlines may jointly operate a connecting flight, so ask if your airline operates every segment—you may find that your preferred carrier flies you only part of the way. International flights on a country's flag carrier are almost always nonstop; U.S. airlines often fly direct.

➤ MAJOR AIRLINES: **American Airlines** (☎ 800/433–7300 in the U.S., 876/952–5950 in Montego Bay, 876/924–8305 in Kingston) flies nonstop daily from New York, Miami, and San Juan, Puerto Rico. **Continental** (☎ 800/231–0856 in the U.S., 876/952–4495 in Montego Bay) flies in four times a week from Newark. **Northwest Airlines** (☎ 800/447–4747 in the U.S., 876/952–9740 in Montego Bay) has daily direct service to Montego Bay from Minneapolis and Tampa. **US Airways** (☎ 800/842–5374 in the U.S., 876/929–9020 in Kingston) flies in from Baltimore and Charlotte.

➤ SMALLER AIRLINES: **Air Jamaica** (☎ 800/523–5585, 876/952–4100 in Montego Bay, 876/922–4661 in Kingston) provides the most frequent service from U.S. cities, including Atlanta, Baltimore, Chicago, Fort Lauderdale, Los Angeles, Miami, New York, Orlando, Philadelphia, and San Francisco. Panamanian carrier **Copa** (☎ 876/926–1762) offers service between Miami and Kingston. **Cubana** (☎ 876/978–3410) flies in from Havana.

➤ FROM CANADA: **Air Canada** (☎ 800/776–3000; 876/952–5160 in Montego Bay, 876/942–8211 in Kingston) offers daily service from Toronto, Halifax, Winnipeg, and Montréal in conjunction with Air Jamaica.

➤ FROM THE U.K.: **Air Jamaica** (☎ 0181/570–7999). **British Airways** (☎ 0345/222–111 in the U.K., 876/952–3771 in Montego Bay, 876/929–9020 in Kingston).

➤ AIR TRAVEL WITHIN JAMAICA: **Air Jamaica Express** (☎ 876/952–5401 in Montego Bay, 876/923–8680 in Kingston), a new subsidiary of Air Jamaica, provides shuttle services on the island. Be sure to reconfirm your departing flight a full 72 hours in advance. Shuttle service between Montego Bay, Ocho Rios, and Negril is now available from **Air SuperClub** (☎ 876/940–7746). **Tropical Airlines** (☎ 876/968–2473 in Kingston, 876/979–3565 in Montego Bay) offers service between Kingston and Montego Bay as well as Cuba.

CHARTERS

Charters usually have the lowest fares but are the least dependable. Departures are infrequent and seldom on time, flights can be delayed for up to 48 hours or can be canceled for any reason up to 10 days before you're scheduled to leave. Itineraries and prices can change after you've booked your flight.

In the U.S., the Department of Transportation's (DOT's) Aviation Consumer Protection Division has jurisdiction over charters and provides some protection. The DOT requires that money paid to charter operators be held in escrow, so if you can't pay with a credit card, **always make your check payable to a charter carrier's escrow account.** The name of the bank should be in the charter contract. If you have any problems with a charter operator, contact the DOT (☞ Airline Complaints, *below*). If you buy a charter package that includes both air and land arrangements, remember that the escrow requirement applies only to the air component.

CHECK IN & BOARDING

Airlines routinely overbook planes, assuming that not everyone with a ticket will show up, but sometimes everyone does. When that happens, airlines ask for volunteers to give up their seats. In return these volunteers usually get a certificate for a free flight and are rebooked on the next flight out. If there aren't enough volunteers, the airline must choose who will be denied boarding. The first to get bumped are passengers who checked in late and those flying on discounted tickets, so **get to the gate, and check in as early as possible,** especially during peak periods.

Although the trend on international flights is to drop reconfirmation requirements, many airlines still ask you to reconfirm each leg of your international itinerary. Failure to do so may result in your reservation being canceled.

Always **bring a government-issued photo ID to the airport.** You may be asked to show it before you are allowed to check in.

CONSOLIDATORS

Consolidators buy tickets for scheduled international flights at reduced rates from the airlines, then sell them at prices that beat the best fare available directly from the airlines, usually without restrictions. Sometimes you can even get your money back if you need to return the ticket. Carefully read the fine print detailing penalties for changes and cancellations, and **confirm your consolidator reservation with the airline.**

➤ CONSOLIDATORS: **Cheap Tickets** (☏ 800/377–1000). **Discount Travel Network** (☏ 800/576–1600). **Unitravel** (☏ 800/325–2222). **Up & Away Travel** (☏ 212/889–2345). **World Travel Network** (☏ 800/409–6753).

CUTTING COSTS

The least-expensive airfares to the Caribbean are priced for round-trip travel and usually must be purchased in advance. It's smart to **call a number of airlines, and when you're quoted a good price, book it on the spot**—the same fare may not be available the next day.

Airlines generally allow you to change your return date for a fee. If you don't use your ticket, you can apply the cost toward the purchase of a new ticket, again for a small charge. However, most low-fare tickets are nonrefundable. To get the lowest airfare, **check different routings.** Compare prices of flights to and from different airports if your destination or home city has more than one gateway. Also price off-peak flights, which may be significantly less expensive.

Travel agents, especially those who specialize in finding the lowest fares (☞ Discounts & Deals, *below*), can be especially helpful when booking a plane ticket. When you're quoted a price, **ask your agent if the price is likely to get any lower.** Good agents know the seasonal fluctuations of airfares and can usually anticipate a sale or fare war. However, waiting can be risky: The fare could go *up* as seats become scarce, and you may wait so long that your preferred flight sells out. A wait-and-see strategy works best if your plans are flexible. If you must arrive and depart on certain dates, don't delay.

DISCOUNT PASSES

Air Jamaica (☏ 800/523–5585) has an island-hopping program: If you stay over in Jamaica, you can fly to a second or even a third destination for free.

FLYING TIMES

The flying time from Los Angeles is about 5½ hours; from New York about 3½ hours; from Miami, about 1 hour.

HOW TO COMPLAIN

If your baggage goes astray or your flight goes awry, complain right away. Most carriers require that you **file a claim immediately.**

➤ AIRLINE COMPLAINTS: DOT Aviation Consumer Protection Division (✉ C-75, Room 4107, Washington, DC 20590, ☎ 202/366–2220). **Federal Aviation Administration (FAA) Consumer Hotline** (☎ 800/322–7873).

AIRPORTS

Donald Sangster International Airport (☎ 876/952–3124), in Montego Bay, is the most efficient point of entry for visitors destined for Montego Bay, Ocho Rios, Runaway Bay, and Negril. **Norman Manley International Airport** (☎ 876/924–8235), in Kingston, is best for visitors to the capital or Port Antonio.

BICYCLES, MOPEDS, AND MOTORCYCLES

The front desks of most major hotels can arrange the rental of bicycles, mopeds, and motorcycles. Daily rates run from about $45 for a moped to $70 for a Honda 550. Deposits of $100–$300 or more are required. However, **we highly recommend that you *not* rent a moped or motorcy-** **cle.** The strangeness of driving on the left, the less-than-cautious driving style that prevails on the island, the abundance of potholes, and the prevalence of vendors who will approach you at every traffic light are just a few reasons to skip cycles.

BUSES

Buses are the mode of transportation Jamaicans use most, and consequently they're *extremely* crowded and slow. They're also not air-conditioned and rather uncomfortable. Yet the service is fairly frequent between Kingston and Montego Bay and between other significant destinations. Schedule or route information is available at bus stops or from the bus driver.

CAMERAS & COMPUTERS

EQUIPMENT PRECAUTIONS

Always **keep your film, tape, or computer disks out of the sun.** Carry an extra supply of batteries, and **be prepared to turn on your camera, camcorder, or laptop** to prove to security personnel that the device is real. Always **ask for hand inspection of film,** which becomes clouded after successive exposure to airport X-ray machines, and **keep videotapes and computer disks away from metal detectors.**

TRAVEL PHOTOGRAPHY

Capturing frothy waves and palm-lined crescents on film is relatively easy if you keep a few thoughts in mind. **Don't let the brightness of the sun on sand and water fool your light meter.** You'll need to compensate or else work early or late in the day when the light isn't as harsh and contrast isn't such a problem. Try to **capture expansive views**; use a wide-angle lens, and look for vistas where the sea draws your eye into a scene. Consider shooting down onto the shore from a clearing on a hillside or from a rock on the beach.

➤ PHOTO HELP: **Kodak Information Center** (☎ 800/242–2424). *Kodak Guide to Shooting Great Travel Pictures,* available in bookstores or from Fodor's Travel Publications (☎ 800/533–6478; $16.50 plus $4 shipping).

CAR RENTAL

Traffic keeps to the left in Jamaica. Driving in Jamaica is a chore and can be extremely frustrating—**we don't recommend it.** You must constantly be on guard—for enormous potholes, people and animals darting out in the street, and aggressive drivers. Although Jamaica has dozens of car-rental companies (you'll find branches at the airports and the resorts among other places), rentals can be difficult to arrange once you've arrived. **Make reservations and send a deposit before your trip.** (Cars are scarce, and without either a confirmation number or a receipt, you may be out of luck.) To get the best deal,

book through a travel agent who is willing to shop around. Rates average $65–$120 a day. Also **ask your travel agent about a company's customer-service record.** How has the company responded to late plane arrivals and vehicle mishaps? Are there often lines at the rental counter? If you're traveling during a holiday period, does a confirmed reservation guarantee you a car?

INSURANCE

When driving a rented car you're generally responsible for any damage to or loss of the vehicle. You also are liable for any property damage or personal injury that you may cause while driving. Before you rent, **see what coverage you already have** under the terms of your personal auto-insurance policy and credit cards.

REQUIREMENTS

You must be at least 21 years old to rent a car (at least 25 years old at several agencies), have a valid driver's license (from any country), and have a valid credit card. You may be required to post a security of several hundred dollars before taking possession of your car; ask about it when you make the reservation.

SURCHARGES

Some rental agencies charge extra if you return the car before the time specified in your contract. To avoid a hefty refueling fee, **fill the tank just before you turn in the** car, but be aware that gas stations near the rental outlet may overcharge. Gas stations are open daily but accept cash only. Gas costs roughly $1–$1.10 a gallon.

➤ RENTAL AGENCIES: **Avis** (☎ 800/331–1212 or 876/952–4543 in Montego Bay, 876/924–8013 in Kingston), **Budget** (☎ 876/952–3838 in Montego Bay, 876/924–8762 in Kingston), **Hertz** (☎ 800/654–3131 or 876/979–0438 in Montego Bay), **Island Car Rentals** (☎ 876/952–5771 in Montego Bay, 876/926–5991 in Kingston), **Jamaica Car Rental** (☎ 876/952–5586 in Montego Bay, 876/974–2505 in Ocho Rios), or **United Car Rentals** (☎ 876/952–3077).

CHILDREN & TRAVEL

Jamaican resorts are increasingly sensitive to families' needs. Many now have children's programs. The more innovative programs will include island jaunts, ecological awareness studies, and fun, informative classes in local culture and cuisine (hair-braiding, reggae, folktales, and how to cook jerk). Baby food is easy to find, but outside major hotels you may not find such items as high chairs and cribs.

Be sure to plan ahead and **involve your youngsters** as you outline your trip. When packing, include things to keep them busy en route. On sightseeing days try to schedule activities of special interest to your children. If you're renting a car don't forget to **arrange for a car seat** when you reserve.

FLYING

If your children are two or older, **ask about children's airfares.** As a rule, infants under two not occupying a seat fly at greatly reduced fares or even for free.

In general the adult baggage allowance applies to children paying half or more of the adult fare. When booking, **ask about carry-on allowances for those traveling with infants.** In general, for babies charged 10% of the adult fare you're allowed one carry-on bag and a collapsible stroller, which may have to be checked; you may be limited to less if the flight is full.

Experts agree that it's a good idea to use safety seats aloft for children weighing less than 40 pounds. Airlines, however, can set their own policies: U.S. carriers allow FAA-approved models but usually require that you buy a ticket, even if your child would otherwise ride free, since the seats must be strapped into regular seats. Airline rules vary, so it's important to **check your airline's policy about using safety seats during takeoff and landing.** Safety seats cannot obstruct the movement of other passengers in the row, so get an appropriate seat assignment as early as possible.

CONSUMER PROTECTION

Whenever possible, **pay with a major credit card** so you can cancel payment or get reimbursed if there's a problem, provided that you can provide documentation. This is the best way to pay, whether you're buying travel arrangements before your trip or shopping at your destination.

If you're doing business with a particular company for the first time, **contact your local Better Business Bureau and the attorney general's offices** in your state and the company's home state, as well. Have any complaints been filed?

Finally, if you're buying a package or tour, always **consider travel insurance** that includes default coverage (☞ Insurance, *below*).

➤ LOCAL BBBs: **Council of Better Business Bureaus** (✉ 4200 Wilson Blvd., Suite 800, Arlington, VA 22203, ☎ 703/276–0100, FAX 703/525–8277).

CULTURE

FESTIVALS AND SEASONAL EVENTS

The biggest festival is Carnival, an event filled with lots of music and dancing in the streets. It's held in Kingston, Ocho Rios, and Montego Bay every April and in Negril every May. Music lovers also fill the island for the August Reggae Sunsplash International Music Festival, which is getting hotter every year, as the best, brightest, and newest of the reggae stars gather to perform in open-air concerts in Montego Bay. Anglers come to Port Antonio to compete in the annual Blue Marlin Tournament, which is usually held in October.

GOOD READS

Anthony C. Winkler's novels, *The Great Yacht Race, The Lunatic,* and *The Painted Canoe,* provide scathingly witty glimpses into Jamaica's class structure.

LANGUAGE

The official language of Jamaica is English. Islanders usually speak a patois among themselves, a lyrical mixture of English, Spanish, and various African languages. Some examples of patois are *me diyah* (I'm here; pronounced "mee de-ya"), *nyam* (eat; pronounced "yam"), and, if someone asks how your vacation is going, just say *"irie"* (pronounced eye-ree), which means "great."

RASTAFARIANS

As you travel the island, you'll see Rastafarians, identified by their flowing dreadlocks (although some prefer to wear their hair beneath knitted mushroom caps, especially in work situations). Rastas smoke marijuana as part of their religious rites, do not eat salt or pork (many are vegetarians), and often sell crafts. Always ask for permission before taking a photograph; if you purchase an item from a vendor (no matter how small), many will allow a photo if asked politely.

CUSTOMS & DUTIES

When shopping, **keep receipts** for all of your purchases. Upon reentering the country, **be ready to show customs officials what you've bought.** If you feel a duty is incorrect, appeal the assessment. If you object to the way your clearance was handled, get the inspector's badge number. In either case, first ask to see a supervisor, then write to the appropriate authorities, beginning with the port director at your point of entry.

IN THE CARIBBEAN

To allay its concerns about smuggling or drug-running, Jamaica inspects most baggage at customs. If you're yachting through the islands—either bareboat or charter—note that harbor customs are often thorough as well. Generally, similar rules apply throughout the Caribbean: You shouldn't bring more than two liters of alcohol, two cartons of cigarettes, or an inordinate amount of duty-free goods into any country. Just as in reentering the United States, any items over the limit might be confiscated or you'll be asked to pay a hefty import tax.

IN AUSTRALIA

Australia residents who are 18 or older may bring back $A400 worth of souvenirs and gifts (including jewelry), 250 cigarettes or 250 grams of tobacco, and 1,125 ml of alcohol (including wine, beer, and spirits). Residents under 18 may bring back $A200 worth of goods.

➤ INFORMATION: **Australian Customs Service** (Regional Director, ✉ Box 8, Sydney, NSW 2001, ☎ 02/9213–2000, FAX 02/9213–4000).

IN CANADA

Canadian residents who have been out of Canada for at least seven days may bring in C$500 worth of goods duty-free. If you've been away less than seven days but more than 48 hours, the duty-free allowance drops to C$200; if your trip lasts 24–48 hours, the allowance is C$50. You may not pool allowances with family members. Goods claimed under the C$500 exemption may follow you by mail; those claimed under the lesser exemptions must accompany you. Alcohol and tobacco products may be included in the seven-day and 48-hour exemptions but not in the 24-hour exemption. If you meet the age requirements of the province or territory through which you reenter Canada, you may bring in, duty-free, 1.14 liters (40 imperial ounces) of wine or liquor *or* 24 12-ounce cans or bottles of beer or ale. If you're 16 or older you may bring in, duty-free, 200 cigarettes and 50 cigars.

You may send an unlimited number of gifts worth up to C$60 each duty-free to Canada. Label the package UNSOLICITED GIFT—VALUE UNDER $60. Alcohol and tobacco are excluded.

➤ INFORMATION: **Revenue Canada** (✉ 2265 St. Laurent Blvd. S, Ottawa, Ontario K1G 4K3, ☎ 613/993–0534, 800/461–9999 in Canada).

IN NEW ZEALAND

Although greeted with a "Haere Mai" ("Welcome to New Zealand"), homeward-bound residents with goods to declare must present themselves for inspection. If you're 17 or older, you may bring back $700 worth of souvenirs and gifts. Your duty-free allowance also includes 4.5 liters of wine or beer; one 1,125-ml bottle of spirits; and either 200 cigarettes, 250 grams of tobacco, 50 cigars, or a combo of all three up to 250 grams.

➤ INFORMATION: **New Zealand Customs** (✉ Custom House, ✉ 50 Anzac Ave., Box 29, Auckland, New Zealand, ☎ 09/359–6655, or 09/309–2978).

IN THE U.K.

From countries outside the EU, including those covered in this book, you may import, duty-free, 200 cigarettes or 50 cigars; 1 liter of spirits or 2 liters of fortified or sparkling wine or liqueurs; 2 liters of still table wine; 60 milliliters of

perfume; 250 milliliters of toilet water; plus £136 worth of other goods, including gifts and souvenirs.

➤ INFORMATION: **HM Customs and Excise** (✉ Dorset House, ✉ Stamford St., London SE1 9NG, ☎ 0171/202–4227).

IN THE U.S.

U.S. residents may bring home $600 worth of foreign goods duty-free if they've been out of the country for at least 48 hours and haven't used the $600 allowance or any part of it in the past 30 days. This allowance, higher than the standard $400 exemption, applies to two dozen countries included in the Caribbean Basin Initiative (CBI).

U.S. residents 21 and older may bring back 1 liter of alcohol duty-free. In addition, regardless of your age, you're allowed 200 cigarettes and 100 non-Cuban cigars. Antiques, which the U.S. Customs Service defines as objects more than 100 years old, enter duty-free, as do original works of art done entirely by hand, including paintings, drawings, and sculptures.

You may also send packages home duty-free: up to $200 worth of goods for personal use, with a limit of one parcel per addressee per day (and no alcohol or tobacco products or perfume worth more than $5); label the package PERSONAL USE, and attach a list of its contents and their retail value. *Do not* label the package UNSOLICITED GIFT, or your duty-free exemption will drop to $100. Mailed items do not affect your duty-free allowance on your return.

➤ INFORMATION: **U.S. Customs Service** (Inquiries, ✉ Box 7407, Washington, DC 20044, ☎ 202/927–6724; complaints, Office of Regulations and Rulings, ✉ 1301 Constitution Ave. NW, Washington, DC 20229; registration of equipment, Resource Management, ✉ 1301 Constitution Ave. NW, Washington, DC 20229, ☎ 202/927–0540).

DISABILITIES & ACCESSIBILITY

ACCESS IN THE CARIBBEAN

In the Caribbean very few attractions and sights are equipped with ramps, elevators, or wheelchair-accessible rest rooms. However, major properties are planning with the needs of travelers with disabilities in mind. Wherever possible in our lodging listings, we indicate whether special facilities are available.

MAKING RESERVATIONS

When discussing accessibility with an operator or reservations agent, **ask hard questions.** Are there any stairs, inside *or* out? Are there grab bars next to the toilet *and* in the shower/tub? How wide is the doorway to the room? To the bathroom? For the most extensive facilities meeting the latest legal specifications, **opt for newer accommodations,** which are more likely to have been designed with access in mind. Older buildings or ships may have more limited facilities. Be sure to **discuss your needs before booking.**

TRAVEL AGENCIES & TOUR OPERATORS

As a whole, the travel industry has become more aware of the needs of travelers with disabilities. In the United States, the Americans with Disabilities Act requires that travel firms serve the needs of all travelers. Note, though, that some agencies and operators specialize in making travel arrangements for individuals and groups with disabilities.

➤ TRAVELERS WITH MOBILITY PROBLEMS: **Access Adventures** (✉ 206 Chestnut Ridge Rd., Rochester, NY 14624, ☎ 716/889–9096) is run by a former physical-rehabilitation counselor. **Accessible Journeys** (✉ 35 W. Sellers Ave., Ridley Park, PA 19078, ☎ 610/521–0339 or 800/846–4537, FAX 610/521–6959) has escorted tours exclusively for travelers with mobility impairments. **CareVacations** (✉ 5019 49th Ave., Suite 102, Leduc, Alberta T9E 6T5, ☎ 403/986–6404, 800/648–1116 in Canada) has group tours and is especially helpful with cruise vacations. **Flying Wheels Travel** (✉ 143 W. Bridge St., Box 382, Owatonna, MN 55060, ☎ 507/451–5005 or 800/535–6790, FAX 507/451–1685) is a travel agency specializing in customized tours and itineraries worldwide. **Hinsdale Travel Service** (⊠ 201 E. Ogden Ave., Suite 100, Hinsdale, IL 60521, ☎ 630/325–1335) is a travel agency that benefits from the advice of wheelchair traveler Janice Perkins. **Tomorrow's Level of Care** (⊠ Box 470299, Brooklyn, NY 11247, ☎ 718/756–0794 or 800/ 932–2012) offers nursing services and medical equipment.

DISCOUNTS & DEALS

Be a smart shopper and **compare all your options** before making any choice. A plane ticket bought with a promotional coupon may not be cheaper than the least expensive fare from a discount ticket agency. For high-price travel purchases, such as packages or tours, keep in mind that what you get is just as important as what you save. Just because something is cheap doesn't mean it's a bargain.

Consider visiting during the off-season, when prices usually plummet at even the glitziest resorts; you'll realize savings of up to 50% between April 15 and December 15. Moreover, you'll usually find fewer tourists, it's easier to rent a car, the water tends to be calmer and clearer, and you might stumble onto local festivals. Besides the region's traditional low season, the Caribbean has other small "windows" during high season, when hotels that face sharp drops in occupancy quietly lower their rates for a week or so. A common window occurs in early-to-mid January, just after the Christmas rush and before the February surge of visitors. Jamaica tends to be competitive and creative in its package deal pricing. All-inclusives aren't always the bargain they seem, especially if you're not a big drinker. Motorized water sports and scuba diving are rarely included, and island tours are occasionally extra as well. And if you're looking for a tranquil vacation, definitely avoid all-inclusives, many of which have "hospitality" staffers who all but drag you off your beach chair to play water volleyball.

CLUBS & COUPONS

Many companies sell discounts in the form of travel clubs and coupon books, but these cost money. You must use participating advertisers to get a deal, and only after you recoup the initial membership cost or book price do you begin to save. If you plan to use the club or coupons frequently, you may save considerably. Before signing up, find out what discounts you get for free.

➤ DISCOUNT CLUBS: **Entertainment Travel Editions** (⊠ 2125 Butterfield Rd., Troy, MI 48084, ☎ 800/ 445–4137; $20–$51, depending on destination). **Great American Traveler** (⊠ Box 27965, Salt Lake City, UT 84127, ☎ 801/974– 3033 or 800/548–2812; $49.95 per year). **Moment's Notice Discount Travel Club** (⊠ 7301 New

Utrecht Ave., Brooklyn, NY 11204, ☎ 718/234–6295; $25 per year, single or family). **Privilege Card International** (⊠ 237 E. Front St., Youngstown, OH 44503, ☎ 330/746–5211 or 800/ 236–9732; $74.95 per year). **Sears's Mature Outlook** (⊠ Box 9390, Des Moines, IA 50306, ☎ 800/336–6330; $19.95 per year). **Travelers Advantage** (⊠ CUC Travel Service, ⊠ 3033 S. Parker Rd., Suite 1000, Aurora, CO 80014, ☎ 800/548–1116 or 800/ 648–4037; $59.95 per year, single or family). **Worldwide Discount Travel Club** (⊠ 1674 Meridian Ave., Miami Beach, FL 33139, ☎ 305/534–2082; $50 per year family, $40 single).

CREDIT-CARD BENEFITS

When you use your credit card to make travel purchases you may get free travel-accident insurance, collision-damage insurance, and medical or legal assistance, depending on the card and the bank that issued it. American Express, MasterCard, and Visa provide one or more of these services, so **get a copy of your credit card's travel-benefits policy.** If you're a member of an auto club, always **ask hotel and car-rental reservations agents about auto-club discounts.** Some clubs offer additional discounts on tours, cruises, and admission to attractions.

DISCOUNT RESERVATIONS

To save money, **look into discount-reservations services** with toll-free numbers, which use their buying power to get a better price on hotels, airline tickets, even car rentals. When booking a room, always **call the hotel's local toll-free number** (if one is available) rather than the central reservations number—you'll often get a better price. Always ask about special packages or corporate rates.

When shopping for the best deal on hotels and car rentals, **look for guaranteed exchange rates,** which protect you against a falling dollar. With your rate locked in, you won't pay more, even if the price goes up in the local currency.

➤ AIRLINE TICKETS: ☎ 800/FLY–4–LESS.

➤ HOTEL ROOMS: **Steigenberger Reservation Service** (☎ 800/223–5652).

PACKAGE DEALS

Packages and guided tours can save you money, but don't confuse the two. When you buy a package, your travel remains independent, just as though you had planned and booked the trip yourself. Fly/drive packages, which combine airfare and car rental, are often a good deal.

DIVING

For a list of training facilities where you can earn your diving certification card, write to **PADI** (⊠ Professional Association of Diving Instructors, 1251 E. Dyer

Rd., #100, Santa Ana, CA 92705). For more information, *see* Chapter 4.

DIVERS' ALERT
Do not fly within 24 hours after scuba diving.

ELECTRICITY

Like the electrical current in North America, the current in Jamaica is 110 volts/50 cycles with flat, two-prong American outlets. Some hotels provide 220-volt plugs as well as special shaver outlets.

If your appliances are dual-voltage, you'll need only an adapter. Don't use 110-volt outlets, marked FOR SHAVERS ONLY, for high-wattage appliances such as blow-dryers. Most laptops operate equally well on 110 and 220 volts and so require only an adapter.

EMERGENCIES

Air rescue and **police:** ☎ 119. **Ambulance** and **fire department:** ☎ 110. **Hospitals: Cornwall Regional Hospital** (⊠ Mt. Salem, Montego Bay, ☎ 876/952–5100), **Port Antonio General Hospital** (⊠ Naylor's Hill, Port Antonio, ☎ 876/993–2646), **St. Ann's Bay Hospital** (⊠ St. Ann's Bay, ☎ 876/972–0150), which has a hyperbaric chamber for scuba diving emergencies, and **University Hospital** (⊠ Mona, Kingston, ☎ 876/927–1620). **Pharmacies: Great House Pharmacy** (⊠ Brown's Plaza, Ocho Rios, ☎ 876/974–2352), **Le Méridien Jamaica Pegasus hotel** (⊠ 81 Knutsford Blvd., Kingston, ☎ 876/926–3690), and **McKenzie's Drug Store** (⊠ 16 Strand St., Montego Bay, ☎ 876/952–2467).

GAY & LESBIAN TRAVEL

The Caribbean is not one of the world's gay/lesbian-friendliest destinations. To a certain extent, nearly every island frowns upon same-sex couples strolling hand-in-hand down a beach or street. Couples may want to request a king-size bed in advance to avoid misunderstandings.

➤ GAY- AND LESBIAN-FRIENDLY TRAVEL AGENCIES: **Corniche Travel** (⊠ 8721 Sunset Blvd., Suite 200, West Hollywood, CA 90069, ☎ 310/854–6000 or 800/429–8747, ℻ 310/659–7441). **Islanders Kennedy Travel** (⊠ 183 W. 10th St., New York, NY 10014, ☎ 212/242–3222 or 800/988–1181, ℻ 212/929–8530). **Now Voyager** (⊠ 4406 18th St., San Francisco, CA 94114, ☎ 415/626–1169 or 800/255–6951, ℻ 415/626–8626). **Yellowbrick Road** (⊠ 1500 W. Balmoral Ave., Chicago, IL 60640, ☎ 773/561–1800 or 800/642–2488, ℻ 773/561–4497). **Skylink Travel and Tour** (⊠ 3577 Moorland Ave., Santa Rosa, CA 95407, ☎ 707/585–8355 or 800/225–5759, ℻ 707/584–5637) serves lesbian travelers.

HEALTH

There are few real hazards. The small lizards that seem to have overrun the islands are harmless, and poisonous snakes are hard to find. Obviously, don't eat unfamiliar berries or leaves, unless you're on a nature walk with an experienced guide. You may want to **bring along a good insect repellent.**

Sunburn or sunstroke can be serious. A long-sleeve shirt, a hat, and long pants or a beach wrap are essential on a boat, for midday at the beach, and whenever you go out sightseeing. **Use sunscreen** with an SPF (sun protection factor) of at least 15—especially if you're fair—and apply it liberally on nose, ears, and other sensitive areas. **Make sure the sunscreen is waterproof** if you're engaging in water sports, **limit your sun time** for the first few days, and be sure to **drink enough liquids,** monitoring intake of caffeine and alcohol, which hasten the dehydration process. No special shots are required for Caribbean destinations.

INSURANCE

Travel insurance is the best way to **protect yourself against financial loss.** The most useful plan is a comprehensive policy that includes coverage for trip cancellation and interruption, default, trip delay, and medical expenses (with a waiver for preexisting conditions).

Without insurance, you will lose all or most of your money if you cancel your trip, regardless of the reason. Default insurance covers you if your tour operator, airline,

or cruise line goes out of business. Trip-delay covers unforeseen expenses that you may incur due to bad weather or mechanical delays. It's important to compare the fine print regarding trip-delay coverage when comparing policies.

For overseas travel, one of the most important components of travel insurance is its medical coverage. Supplemental health insurance will pick up the cost of your medical bills should you get sick or injured while traveling. U.S. residents should note that Medicare generally does not cover health-care costs outside the United States, nor do many privately issued policies. Residents of the United Kingdom can buy an annual travel-insurance policy valid for most vacations taken during the year in which the coverage is purchased. If you are pregnant or have a preexisting condition, make sure you're covered. British citizens should buy extra medical coverage when traveling overseas, according to the Association of British Insurers. Australian travelers should buy travel insurance, including extra medical coverage, whenever they go abroad, according to the Insurance Council of Australia.

Always **buy travel insurance directly from the insurance company**; if you buy it from a cruise line, airline, or tour operator that goes out of business you probably won't be covered for the agency or operator's default, a major risk. Before you make any purchase, **review your existing health and home-owner's policies** to find out whether they cover expenses incurred while traveling.

➤ TRAVEL INSURERS: In the U.S., **Access America** (⊠ 6600 W. Broad St., Richmond, VA 23230, ☎ 804/285–3300 or 800/284–8300). **Travel Guard International** (⊠ 1145 Clark St., Stevens Point, WI 54481, ☎ 715/345–0505 or 800/826–1300). In Canada, **Mutual of Omaha** (⊠ Travel Division, ⊠ 500 University Ave., Toronto, Ontario M5G 1V8, ☎ 416/598–4083, 800/268–8825 in Canada).

➤ INSURANCE INFORMATION: In the U.K., **Association of British Insurers** (⊠ 51 Gresham St., London EC2V 7HQ, ☎ 0171/600–3333). In Australia, the **Insurance Council of Australia** (☎ 613/9614–1077, FAX 613/9614–7924).

LODGING

Plan ahead and **reserve a room well before you travel to the Caribbean.** If you have reservations but expect to arrive later than 5 PM or 6 PM, tell the management in advance. Unless so advised, some places won't hold your reservations after 6 PM. Also, be sure to **find out what the quoted rate includes**—use of sports facilities and equipment, airport transfers, and the like—and whether the property operates on the European Plan (EP,

with no meals), Continental Plan (CP, with Continental breakfast), Breakfast Plan (BP, with full breakfast), Modified American Plan (MAP, with two meals), or Full American Plan (FAP, with three meals), or is all-inclusive (including three meals, all facilities, and drinks unless otherwise noted). Be sure to **bring your deposit receipt** with you in case questions arise.

Decide whether you want to pay the extra price for a room overlooking the ocean or pool. At slightly less expensive properties, the difference may be as little as $10–$20 per room; at luxury resorts on pricey islands, however, it could be as much as $100 per room. Also **find out how close the property is to a beach**; at some hotels you can walk barefoot from your room onto the sand; others are across a road or a 10-minute drive away. Nighttime entertainment is often alfresco in Jamaica, so if you go to sleep early or are a light sleeper, ask for a room away from the dance floor.

Air-conditioning is not always a necessity due to cooling trade winds, but it can be a plus if you enjoy an afternoon snooze. Breezes are best in second-floor rooms, particularly corner rooms. If you like to sleep without air-conditioning, make sure that windows can be opened and have screens. If you're staying away from the water, make sure the room has a ceiling fan, and that it works.

If you're concerned about the possibility of a hurricane ruining your vacation, the Sandals chain has a "Blue Chip Ultra Hurricane Guarantee" that will replace the cost of your vacation if one affects your trip. Contact a Sandals hotel for details (☞ Chapter 2).

In this book, we categorize properties by price. Prices are intended as a guideline only.

APARTMENT & VILLA RENTALS

If you want a home base that's roomy enough for a family and comes with cooking facilities, **consider a furnished rental.** These can save you money, especially if you're traveling with a large group of people. Home-exchange directories list rentals (often second homes owned by prospective house swappers), and some services search for a house or apartment for you and handle the paperwork. Some send an illustrated catalog; others send photographs only of specific properties, sometimes at a charge. Up-front registration fees may apply.

➤ RENTAL AGENTS: **At Home Abroad** (⊠ 405 E. 56th St., Suite 6H, New York, NY 10022, ☎ 212/421–9165, ☒ 212/752–1591). **Europa-Let/Tropical Inn-Let** (⊠ 92 N. Main St., Ashland, OR 97520, ☎ 541/482–5806 or 800/462–4486, ☒ 541/482–

0660). **Hideaways International** (⊠ 767 Islington St., Portsmouth, NH 03801, ☎ 603/430–4433 or 800/843–4433, ☒ 603/430–4444; membership $99) is a club for travelers who arrange rentals among themselves.

Property Rentals International (⊠ 1008 Mansfield Crossing Rd., Richmond, VA 23236, ☎ 804/378–6054 or 800/220–3332, ☒ 804/379–2073). **Unusual Villa & Island Rentals** (⊠ 409F North Hamilton St., Richmond, VA 23221, ☎ 804/288–2823, ☒ 804/342–9016). **Vacation Home Rentals Worldwide** (⊠ 235 Kensington Ave., Norwood, NJ 07648, ☎ 201/767–9393 or 800/633–3284, ☒ 201/767–5510). **Villas and Apartments Abroad** (⊠ 420 Madison Ave., Suite 1003, New York, NY 10017, ☎ 212/759–1025 or 800/433–3020, ☒ 212/755–8316). **Villas International** (⊠ 950 Northgate Dr., Suite 206, San Rafael, CA 94903, ☎ 415/499–9490 or 800/221–2260, ☒ 415/499–9491).

MONEY

The official currency is the Jamaican dollar. At press time the exchange rate was about J$35 to US$1. U.S. money (currency only, no coins) is accepted at most establishments, although you'll often be given change in Jamaican money. **ATM machines do not accept American bank cards,** although cash advances can be made using credit cards. Note that prices quoted throughout this book are in U.S. dollars unless otherwise noted.

CREDIT & DEBIT CARDS

Should you use a credit card or a debit card when traveling? Both have benefits. A credit card allows you to delay payment and gives you certain rights as a consumer (☞ Consumer Protection, *above*). A debit card, also known as a check card, deducts funds directly from your checking account and helps you stay within your budget. When you want to rent a car, though, you may still need an old-fashioned credit card. Although you can always *pay* for your car with a debit card, some agencies will not allow you to *reserve* a car with a debit card.

Otherwise, the two types of plastic are virtually the same. Both will get you cash advances at ATMs worldwide if your card is properly programmed with your personal identification number (PIN). Both offer excellent, wholesale exchange rates. And both protect you against unauthorized use if the card is lost or stolen. Your liability is limited to $50, as long as you report the card missing.

➤ ATM LOCATIONS: **Cirrus** (☎ 800/424–7787). **Plus** (☎ 800/843–7587) for locations in the U.S. and Canada, or visit your local bank.

EXCHANGING MONEY

For the most favorable rates, **change money through banks.** Although fees charged for ATM transactions may be higher abroad than at home, Cirrus and Plus exchange rates are excellent, because they are based on wholesale rates offered only by major banks. You won't do as well at exchange booths in airports or rail and bus stations, in hotels, in restaurants, or in stores, although you may find their hours more convenient. To avoid lines at airport exchange booths, **get a bit of local currency before you leave home.**

➤ EXCHANGE SERVICES: **Chase *Currency To Go*** (☎ 800/935–9935; 935–9935 in NY, NJ, and CT). **International Currency Express** (☎ 888/842–0880 on the East Coast, 888/278–6628 on the West Coast). **Thomas Cook Currency Services** (☎ 800/287–7362 for telephone orders and retail locations).

SERVICE CHARGES, TAXES, AND TIPPING

Most hotels and restaurants add a 10% service charge to your bill. Hotels collect a 10% government consumption tax on room occupancy. When a service charge isn't included, a 10% to 20% tip is appreciated. Tips of 10% to 20% are customary for taxi drivers as well.

TRAVELER'S CHECKS

Do you need traveler's checks? It depends on where you're headed. If you're going to rural areas and small towns, go with cash; traveler's checks are best used in cities. Lost or stolen checks can usually be replaced within 24 hours. To ensure a speedy refund, buy your own traveler's checks—don't let someone else pay for them: irregularities like this can cause delays. The person who bought the checks should make the call to request a refund.

OPENING AND CLOSING TIMES

Normal business hours for stores are weekdays 8:30–4:30, Saturday 8–1. Banks are generally open Monday–Thursday 9–2, Friday 9–4. Post offices are open weekdays 9–5.

PACKING

LUGGAGE

How many carry-on bags you can bring with you is up to the airline. Most allow two, but the limit is often reduced to one on certain flights. Gate agents will take excess baggage—including bags they deem oversize—from you as you board and add it to checked luggage. To avoid this situation, make sure that everything you carry aboard will fit under your seat.

Airline liability for baggage is limited to $1,250 per person on flights within the United States. On international flights it amounts to $9.07 per pound or $20 per kilogram for checked baggage (roughly $640 per 70-pound bag) and $400 per passenger for unchecked baggage. You can buy additional coverage at check-in for about $10 per $1,000 of coverage, but it excludes a rather extensive list of items, shown on your airline ticket.

Before departure, **itemize your bags' contents** and their worth, and label the bags with your name, address, and phone number. (If you use your home address, cover it so that potential thieves can't see it readily.) Inside each bag, **pack a copy of your itinerary.** At check-in, **make sure that each bag is correctly tagged** with the destination airport's three-letter code. If your bags arrive damaged or fail to arrive at all, file a written report with the airline before leaving the airport.

PACKING LIST

Dress in Jamaica is light and casual. Bring loose-fitting clothes made of natural fabrics to see you through days of heat and humidity. Take a cover-up for the beaches, not only to protect you from the sun but also to wear to and from your hotel room. Bathing suits and immodest attire are frowned upon off the beach on many islands. A sun hat is advisable, but you don't have to pack one—inexpensive straw hats are available everywhere. For shopping and sightseeing, bring walking shorts, jeans, T-shirts, long-sleeve cotton shirts, slacks, and sundresses. You'll need a light sweater for protection from the trade winds, and at higher altitudes. Evenings are casual, but "casual" can range from really informal to casually elegant, depending on the establishment. A tie is rarely required, but jackets are sometimes de rigueur in fancier restaurants.

In your carry-on luggage **bring an extra pair of eyeglasses or contact lenses and enough of any medication** to last the entire trip. You may also want your doctor to write a spare prescription using the drug's generic name, since brand names may vary from country to country. **Never put prescription drugs or valuables in luggage to be checked.** To avoid customs delays, carry medications in their original packaging. And don't forget to copy down and carry addresses of offices that handle refunds of lost traveler's checks.

PASSPORTS & VISAS

When traveling internationally make **two photocopies of your passport's data page** (one for someone at home and another for you, carried separately from your passport). If you lose your passport, promptly call the nearest embassy or consulate and the local police.

ENTERING JAMAICA

Australian, Canadian, New Zealand, U.K., and U.S. citizens all must have a valid passport (for Canadians and Americans, not expired more than one year) and possess a return or ongoing ticket. Declaration forms are distributed in flight to keep customs formalities to a minimum.

PASSPORT OFFICES

The best time to apply for a passport or to renew is during the fall and winter. Before any trip, be sure to check your passport's expiration date and, if necessary, renew it as soon as possible. (Some countries won't allow you to enter on a passport that's due to expire in six months or less.)

➤ AUSTRALIAN CITIZENS: **Australian Passport Office** (☎ 131–232).

➤ CANADIAN CITIZENS: **Passport Office** (☎ 819/994–3500 or 800/567–6868).

➤ NEW ZEALAND CITIZENS: **New Zealand Passport Office** (☎ 04/494–0700 for information on how to apply, 0800/727–776 for information on applications already submitted).

➤ U.K. CITIZENS: **London Passport Office** (☎ 0990/21010), for fees and documentation requirements and to request an emergency passport.

➤ U.S. CITIZENS: **National Passport Information Center** (☎ 900/225–5674; calls are charged at 35¢ per minute for automated service, $1.05 per minute for operator service).

SAFETY

Do not let the beauty of Jamaica cause you to relax the caution and good sense you would use in any unfamiliar place. Never leave valuables in your room; use the safe-deposit boxes that most hotels make available. Carry your funds in traveler's checks and keep a record of the check numbers in a secure place. Never leave a rental car unlocked, and never leave valuables in a locked car. Finally, resist the call of the wild when it presents itself as a scruffy-looking local who offers to show you the "real" Jamaica. Jamaica on the beaten path is wonderful enough; don't take chances by wandering far from it. And ignore efforts, however persistent, to sell you ganja (marijuana). Independent travelers, especially those renting cars, need to take special precautions. Some travelers have been harassed by locals offering to "guard" cars and have experienced vandalism when requests for money were denied. Taxi travel, using the services of knowledgeable, certified taxi drivers, is highly recommended.

SENIOR-CITIZEN TRAVEL

To qualify for age-related discounts, **mention your senior-citizen status up front** when booking hotel reservations (not when checking out) and before you're seated in restaurants (not when paying the bill). Note that discounts may be limited to certain menus, days, or hours. When renting a car, **ask about promotional car-rental discounts,** which can be cheaper than senior-citizen rates.

STUDENT TRAVEL

The Caribbean is not as far out of a student's budget as you might expect. Jamaica has a large resident international student population. In many cases, your student ID card may provide access to university facilities, from library to cafeteria.

TRAVEL AGENCIES

To save money, **look into deals available through student-oriented travel agencies.** To qualify you'll need a bona fide student ID card. Members of international student groups are also eligible.

➤ STUDENT IDS & SERVICES: **Council on International Educational Exchange** (⊠ CIEE, ⊠ 205 E. 42nd St., 14th floor, New York, NY 10017, ☎ 212/822–2600 or 888/268–6245, ℻ 212/822–2699), for mail orders only, in the United States. **Travel Cuts** (⊠ 187 College St., Toronto, Ontario M5T 1P7, ☎ 416/979–2406 or 800/667–2887) in Canada.

TAXIS

Some but not all of Jamaica's taxis are metered. If you accept a driver's offer of his services as a tour guide, be sure to agree on a price before the vehicle is put into gear. All licensed taxis display red Public Passenger Vehicle (PPV) plates. Cabs can be summoned by telephone or flagged down on the street. Rates are per car, not per passenger, and 25% is added to the metered rate between midnight and 5 AM. Licensed minivans are also available and bear the red PPV plates. JUTA is the largest taxi franchise and has offices in all resort areas.

TELEPHONES AND MAIL

To dial Jamaica from the US, just dial 1 + the area code 876 (recently changed from 809). Most hotels offer direct-dial telephone services; local businesses provide telegraph and fax services for a fee. Some U.S. telephone companies, such as MCI, will not permit card calls to be placed from Jamaica due to recent fraud cases. The best option is to purchase a phone card, which are sold in most stores across the island. Calls from town to town are long distance. Pay phones are available in most communities.

Postcards may be mailed anywhere in the world for 90¢ Jamaican; letters to the United States and Canada cost J$10; to Europe, J$12.50.

INTERNATIONAL CALLS

AT&T, and Sprint international access codes make calling the United States relatively convenient, but you may find the local access number blocked in many hotel rooms. First ask the hotel operator to connect you. If the hotel operator balks, ask for an international operator, or dial the international operator yourself. One way to improve your odds of getting connected to your long-distance carrier is to travel with more than one company's calling card (remember that MCI doesn't permit card calls above). If all else fails, call from a pay phone in the hotel lobby. Call your long-distance carrier for a list of access codes on the islands you plan to visit.

➤ ACCESS CODES: **AT&T Direct** (☎ 800/435–0812). **Sprint International Access** (☎ 800/877–4646).

TOUR OPERATORS

Buying a prepackaged tour or independent vacation can make your trip to Jamaica less expensive and more hassle-free. Because everything is prearranged, you'll spend less time planning.

Operators that handle several hundred thousand travelers per year can use their purchasing power to give you a good price. Their high volume may also indicate financial stability. But some small companies provide more personalized service; because they tend to specialize, they may also be more knowledgeable about a given area.

BOOKING WITH AN AGENT

Travel agents are excellent resources. In fact, large operators accept bookings made only through travel agents. But it's a good idea to **collect brochures from several agencies,** because some agents' suggestions may be influenced by relationships with tour and package firms that reward them for volume sales. If you have a special interest, **find an agent with expertise in that area**; the American Society of Travel Agents (☞ Travel Agencies, *below*) has a database of specialists worldwide.

Make sure your travel agent knows the accommodations and other services. Ask about the hotel's location, room size, beds, and whether it has a pool, room service, or programs for children, if you care about these. Has your agent been there in person or sent others you can contact?

Do some homework on your own, too: Local tourism boards can provide information about lesser-known and small-niche operators, some of which may sell only direct.

BUYER BEWARE

Each year consumers are stranded or lose their money when tour operators—even very large ones with excellent reputations—go out of business. So **check out the operator.** Find out how long the company has been in business, and ask several travel agents about its reputation. If the package or tour you are considering is priced lower than in your wildest dreams, **be skeptical.** Try to **book with a company that has a consumer-protection program.** If the operator has such a program, you'll find information about it in the company's brochure. If the operator you are considering does not offer some kind of consumer protection, then ask for references from satisfied customers.

In the United States, members of the National Tour Association and United States Tour Operators Association are required to set aside funds to cover your payments and travel arrangements in case the company defaults. It's also a good idea to choose a company that participates in the American Society of Travel Agent's Tour Operator Program (TOP). This gives you a forum if there are any disputes between you and your tour operator; ASTA will act as mediator.

➤ TOUR-OPERATOR RECOMMENDATIONS: **American Society of Travel Agents** (☞ Travel Agencies, *below*). **National Tour Association** (✉ NTA, ✉ 546 E. Main St., Lexington, KY 40508, ☎ 606/226–4444 or 800/755–8687). **United States Tour Operators Association** (✉ USTOA, ✉ 342 Madison Ave., Suite 1522, New York, NY 10173, ☎ 212/599–6599 or 800/468–7862, ℻ 212/599–6744).

PACKAGES

Independent vacation packages are available from major tour operators and airlines. The companies listed below offer vacation packages in a broad price range.

➤ AIR/HOTEL: **American Airlines Vacations** (☎ 800/321–2121). **Certified Vacations** (☎ 954/522–1440 or 800/233–7260). **Continental Airlines Vacations** (☎ 800/634–5555). **US Airways Vacations** (☎ 800/455–0123).

➤ FROM THE U.K.: **Caribbean Connection** (✉ Concorde House, Forest St., Chester CH1 1QR, ☎ 01244/341–131). **Caribtours** (✉ 161 Fulham Rd., London SW3 6SN, ☎ 0171/581–3517). **Hayes and Jarvis** (✉ Hayes House, 152 King St., London W6 0QA, ☎ 0181/748–0088). **Kuoni Travel** (✉ Kuoni House, Dorking, Surrey RH5 4AZ, ☎ 01306/740–888).

THEME TRIPS

➤ ADVENTURE: **American Wilderness Experience** (✉ Box 1486, Boulder, CO 80306, ☎ 303/444–2622 or 800/444–0099, FAX 303/444–3999). **NatureQuest** (✉ 934 Acapulco St., Laguna Beach, CA 92651, ☎ 714/499–9561 or 800/369–3033, FAX 714/499–0812).

➤ GOLF: **Stine's Golftrips** (✉ Box 2314, Winter Haven, FL 33883-2314, ☎ 407/933–0032 or 800/428–1940, FAX 407/933–8857).

➤ SCUBA DIVING: **Rothschild Dive Safaris** (✉ 900 West End Ave., #1B, New York, NY 10025-3525, ☎ 212/662–4858 or 800/359–0747, FAX 212/749–6172). **Tropical Adventures** (✉ 111 2nd Ave. N, Seattle, WA 98109, ☎ 206/441–3483 or 800/247–3483, FAX 206/441–5431).

➤ YACHT CHARTERS: **Alden Yacht Charters** (✉ 1909 Alden Landing, Portsmouth, RI 02871, ☎ 401/683–4200 or 800/253–3654, FAX 401/683–3668). **Huntley Yacht Vacations** (✉ 210 Preston Rd., Wernersville, PA 19565, ☎ 610/678–2628 or 800/322–9224, FAX 610/670–1767). **Lynn Jachney Charters** (✉ Box 302, Marblehead, MA 01945, ☎ 617/639–0787 or 800/223–2050, FAX 617/639–0216). **The Moorings** (✉ 19345 U.S. Hwy. 19 N, 4th floor, Clearwater, FL 33764, ☎ 813/530–5424 or 800/535–7289, FAX 813/530–9747). **Nicholson Yacht Charters** (✉ 29 Sherman St., Cambridge, MA 02138, ☎ 617/661–0555 or 800/662–6066, FAX 617/661–0554). **Ocean Voyages** (✉ 1709 Bridgeway, Sausalito, CA 94965, ☎ 415/332–4681, FAX 415/332–7460). **Russell Yacht Charters** (✉ 404 Hulls Hwy., #175, Southport, CT 06490, ☎ 203/255–2783 or 800/635–8895). **SailAway Yacht Charter Consultants** (✉ 15605 S.W. 92nd Ave., Miami, FL 33157-1972, ☎ 305/253–7245 or 800/724–5292, FAX 305/251–4408).

TRAVEL AGENCIES

A good travel agent puts your needs first. Look for an agency that has been in business at least five years, emphasizes customer service, and has someone on staff who specializes in your destination. In addition, **make sure the agency belongs to a professional trade organization,** such as the American Society of Travel Agents in the United States. If your travel agency is also acting as your tour operator, *see* Buyer Beware *in* Tour Operators, *above*.

➤ LOCAL AGENT REFERRALS: **American Society of Travel Agents** (ASTA, ☎ 800/965–2782 24-hr hot line, FAX 703/684–8319). **Association of Canadian Travel Agents** (✉ 1729 Bank St., Suite 201, Ottawa, Ontario K1V 7Z5, ☎ 613/521–0474, FAX 613/521–0805). **Association of British Travel Agents** (✉ 55–57 Newman St., London W1P 4AH, ☎ 0171/637–2444, FAX 0171/637–0713). **Australian Federation of Travel Agents** (☎ 02/9264–3299). **Travel Agents' Association of New Zealand** (☎ 04/499–0104).

VISITOR INFORMATION

U.S.–based tourist boards are good sources of general information, up-to-date calendars of events, and listings of hotels, restaurants, sights, and shops. While on island, the Jamaica Tourist Board offers a help line (☎ 888/995–9999) in addition to its offices.

If you'd like to delve into the heart of Jamaica rather than simply explore her sybaritic pleasures, the tourist board can arrange for you to spend time with a local host family through the **Meet the People** program. They'll try to match interests, vocations, ages, whatever, so you'll have common ground. There's no fee involved (other than for activities you and your hosts might select); this is the best way to come to know the warmth and companionship the island has to offer.

➤ IN THE U.S.: **Jamaica Tourist Board** (✉ 801 2nd Ave., 20th floor, New York, NY 10017, ☎ 212/856–9727 or 800/233–4582, www.jamaicatravel.com; ✉ 500 N. Michigan Ave., Suite 1030, Chicago, IL 60611, ☎ 312/527–1296; ✉ 1320 S. Dixie Hwy., Suite 1100, Coral Gables, FL 33146, ☎ 305/665–0557; ✉ 3440 Wilshire Blvd., Suite 805, Los Angeles, CA 90010, ☎ 213/384–1123); **Caribbean Tourism Organization** (✉ 20 E. 46th St., New York, NY 10017-2452, ☎ 212/682–0435, FAX 212/697–4258).

➤ IN CANADA: **Jamaica Tourist Board** (✉ 1 Eglinton Ave. E, Suite 616, Toronto, Ontario M4P 3A1, ☎ 416/482–7850).

➤ IN THE U.K.: **Jamaica Tourist Board** (✉ 1–2 Prince Consort Rd., London SW7 2BZ, ☎ 0171/224–0505). **Caribbean Tourism Organization** (✉ Vigilant House, 120 Wilton Rd., London SW1V 1JZ, England, ☎ 0171/233–8382).

➤ IN JAMAICA: The **Jamaica Tourist Board** (JTB) is in Kingston (✉ 2 St. Lucia Ave., Box 360, Kingston 5, New Kingston, ☎ 876/929–9200). There are also JTB desks at both Montego Bay and Kingston airports and offices in Black River (✉ Hendriks Bldg., 2 High St., ☎ 876/965–2074), Montego Bay (✉ Cornwall Beach, ☎ 876/952–4425), Negril (✉ Coral Seas Plaza, ☎ 876/957–4243), Ocho Rios (✉ Ocean Village Shopping Centre, ☎ 876/974–2570), and Port Antonio (✉ City Centre Plaza, ☎ 876/993–3051).

WHEN TO GO

For information on high and low seasons, *see* Discounts & Deals.

CLIMATE

The Caribbean climate is fairly constant. The average year-round temperatures for the region are 78°F–88°F. The extremes of temperature are 65°F low, 95°F high, but as everyone knows, it's the humidity, not the heat, that makes you suffer, especially when the two go hand in hand. You can count on downtown shopping areas being hot at midday any time of the year, but air-conditioning provides some respite. Stay near beaches, where water and trade winds can keep you cool, and shop early or late in the day.

As part of the fall's rainy season, hurricanes occasionally sweep through the Caribbean. Check the news daily, and keep abreast of brewing tropical storms by reading stateside papers if you can get them. The rainy season consists mostly of brief showers interspersed with sunshine. You can watch the clouds come over, feel the rain, and remain on your lounge chair for the sun to dry you off. A spell of overcast days is "unusual," as everyone will tell you.

High places can be cool, particularly when the Christmas winds hit Caribbean peaks (they come in late November and last through January). Since Jamaica is mountainous, the altitude always offers an escape from the latitude. Kingston swelters in summer, but climb 1,000 ft or so and everything is fine.

1 Destination: Jamaica

THE TAPESTRY OF JAMAICA

AROUND ONE BEND of the winding North Coast Highway lies a palatial home; around another, a shanty without doors or windows. Towns are centers of frenetic activity, filled with pedestrians, street vendors, and neighbors taking time to visit. Roads are crammed with vehicles and full of honking—not a chorus of hostility but notes of greeting or of friendly caution and just for the heck of it. Drivers wait patiently for groups of uniformed schoolchildren and housewives bearing loads on their heads to cross, and a spirit of cooperation prevails among chaos.

A sense of paradox infuses Jamaica, and the first-time visitor is likely to experience a bewildering array of extremes. The maniacal pace on the nation's highways belies a saintly patience and old-fashioned courtliness in other situations. A shockingly high crime rate is countered with openhanded generosity. Decrepit schools mask one of the highest literacy rates in the hemisphere, and the number of rum shops is surpassed only by the number of churches.

The cultural life of Jamaica is a wealthy one; its music, art, and cuisine have a spirit that's easy to sense but as hard to describe as the rhythms of reggae or an outburst of streetwise patois. Although 95% of the population traces its bloodlines to Africa, Jamaica is a stockpot of cultures, including those of other Caribbean islands, Great Britain, the Middle East, India, China, Germany, Portugal, and South America. The third largest island in the Caribbean (after Cuba and Hispaniola), Jamaica enjoys a considerable self-sufficiency based on tourism, agriculture, and mining.

Jamaica's physical attractions include jungle mountaintops, clear waterfalls, and unforgettable beaches, and its tourist areas are grouped around the island's northern and western coastlines. Ocho Rios is a major cruise port, resort center, and the home of Dunn's River Falls, probably the most photographed spot in the nation. Montego Bay, destination of most tourist flights, is a sprawling blend of opulent beach resorts and commerce. At the island's western tip lies Negril, once a sleepy hangout for bohemian travelers, and, though now bigger and glitzier, still a haven for the hip and the hedonistic. In addition to these pleasure capitals, Jamaica has a real capital in Kingston. For all its congestion and for all the disparity between city life and the bikinis and parasails to the north, Kingston is the true heart and head of the island. This is where politics, literature, music, and art wrestle for acceptance in the largest (800,000 people) English-speaking city south of Miami.

If you want to experience Jamaica in its entirety, budget your time carefully. While driving distances may not be great, roads are narrow and winding, and delays are inevitable. However, even a short stay can offer a glimpse of a myriad of attractions that lie within a reasonable distance of the major resort areas.

The first group known to have reached Jamaica were the Arawak Indians, who paddled their canoes from the Orinoco region of South America around AD 1000. In 1494 Christopher Columbus stepped ashore at what is now called Discovery Bay. Having spent four centuries on the island, the Arawaks had little notion that his feet on their sand would mean their extinction within 50 years. What is now St. Ann's Bay was established as New Seville in 1509 and served as the Spanish capital until the local government crossed the is-

land to Santiago de la Vega (now Spanish Town). The Spaniards were never impressed with Jamaica; they found no precious metals, and they let the island fester in poverty for 161 years. When 5,000 British soldiers and sailors appeared in Kingston Harbor in 1655, the Spaniards didn't put up a fight.

The arrival of the English, and the three centuries of rule that followed, provided Jamaica with both the genteel underpinnings of its present life—and a period of history enlivened by a rousing pirate tradition that was fueled by rum. The British buccaneer Henry Morgan counted Jamaica's governor as one of his closest friends and enjoyed the protection of His Majesty's government no matter what he chose to plunder. Port Royal, once said to be the "wickedest city of Christendom," grew up on a spit of land across from present-day Kingston. Morgan and his brigands were delighted to have such a haven, and the people of Jamaica could buy pirate booty at terrific bargains.

Morgan enjoyed a prosperous life; he was knighted and made lieutenant governor of Jamaica before the age of 30, and, like every other good bureaucrat, he died in bed and was given a state funeral. Port Royal fared less well. On June 7, 1692, an earthquake tilted two-thirds of the city into the sea, the tidal wave that followed the last tremors washed away millions in pirate treasure, and Port Royal simply disappeared. In recent years divers have turned up some of the treasure, but most of it still lies in the depths, adding an exotic quality to the water sports pursued along Kingston's reefs.

The very British 18th century was a time of prosperity for landholders in Jamaica. This was the age of the sugar baron, who ruled his plantation great house and made the island the largest sugar-producing colony in the world. Because sugar fortunes were built on slave labor, however, production became less profitable when the Jamaican slave trade was abolished in 1807 and slavery was ended in 1838. Additional labor forces were brought in from India as well as China; wages were low and the economy further diminished. Sugar remained a major export and was later joined by bauxite, mined from the hills to be used in the production of aluminum.

The second half of this century brought independence to Jamaica. On August 6, 1962 the island became an independent nation, although it remains a member of the British Commonwealth. The government is ruled by a freely elected prime minister. Two political parties, the People's National Party (PNP) and the Jamaica Labour Party (JLP), vie for the

position and elections can become heated and even violent events. Election time riots in 1980 resulted in many deaths, mostly in Kingston's ghettos. The late 1997 election was carefully monitored by a contingency that included Jimmy Carter and Colin Powell, and the mood remained peaceful throughout most of the island, despite an economy that includes high unemployment, low wages, and an interest rate that reaches 75 percent.

Today's Jamaica is a place where poverty is rampant and many must work at the fringes of the tourist industry as unlicensed taxi drivers, hair braiders, and vendors who walk the beaches in search of a vacationer. Hassling is one of the most common complaints of travelers to Jamaica, and the government has recently increased fines and even penalties of jail time for this offense. Many problems involve attempts to sell marijuana or ganja, an illegal product.

The smoking of sacramental ganja and flowing dreadlocks are the most recognizable aspect of Rastafarianism, a religion that believes in the divinity of the late Haile Selassie (also known by the name Tafari), progressive emperor of Ethiopia from 1930 to 1974. Rastafarianism began in the 1930s, following the 1920s black pride and nationalist movement led by Jamaican Marcus Garvey, founder of the Universal Negro Improvement Association. Garvey's "back to Africa" message resonated with the Rastas, who embraced Ethiopia as their chosen homeland. Though culture gained strength in the 1960s and became internationally known through celebrities such as the late reggae singer Bob Marley, Rastas are a small sector of the Jamaican population today.

Reggae rhythms are not solely a Rasta musical expression and are just one aspect of Jamaica's rich tapestry. You'll find many subtle melodies on the island, whether that be the sizzle of jerk pork on a roadside grill, the lap of waves on a sandy beach, the call of the tiny doctorbird as it flits through the trees, or the quiet whistle of a breeze through the Blue Mountains.

Jamaica

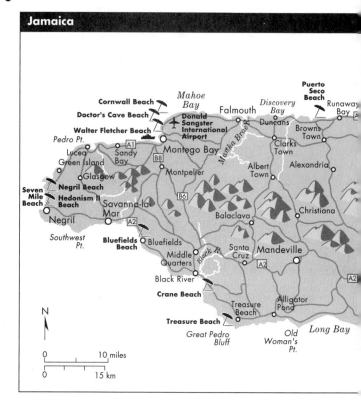

Mahoe Bay

Cornwall Beach

Doctor's Cave Beach

Walter Fletcher Beach

Donald Sangster International Airport

Falmouth

Discovery Bay

Duncans

Runaway Bay

Puerto Seco Beach

Browns Town

Pedro Pt.

Lucea

Green Island

Glasgow

Sandy Bay

Montego Bay

Montpelier

A1

B8

Martha Brae

Clarks Town

Albert Town

Alexandria

Seven Mile Beach

Negril Beach

Hedonism II Beach

Savanna-la-Mar

Negril

Southwest Pt.

Bluefields Beach

Bluefields

Middle Quarters

Black River

B6

Balaclava

Christiana

Mandeville

A2

A2

A2

Santa Cruz

Black R.

Crane Beach

Treasure Beach

Treasure Beach

Alligator Pond

Great Pedro Bluff

Old Woman's Pt.

Long Bay

N

0   10 miles

0   15 km

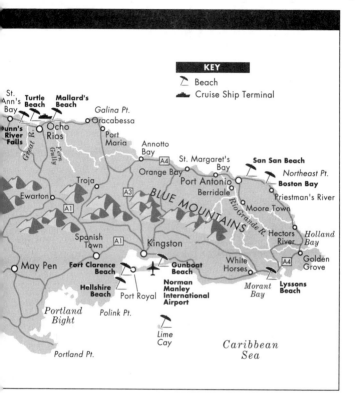

2 Lodging

JAMAICA WAS THE BIRTHPLACE of the Caribbean all-inclusive resort, a concept that took the Club Med idea and gave it an excess-in-the-tropics spin. The all-inclusive is the most popular vacation option in Jamaica, offering incredible values with rates from $145 to $350 per person per night. Prices include airport transfers; accommodations; three meals a day plus snacks; all bar drinks, often including premium liquors; wine, beer, and soft drinks; a plethora of sports, including golf, tennis, aerobics, basketball, boccie, croquet, horseshoes, lawn chess, Ping-Pong, shuffleboard, volleyball, scuba diving, and nonmotorized water sports (instruction and equipment); an array of entertainment options (game rooms with billiards, darts, and/or slot machines; nightclubs; classes in local crafts, cooking, language, and dance; and a showroom or central theater with nightly entertainment); and all gratuities and taxes. The only surcharges are usually for such luxuries as massages, tours, and weddings or vow-renewal ceremonies (though these are often included at high-end all-inclusives). The all-inclusives have branched out, some of them courting families, others going after an upper crust that wouldn't even have picked up a brochure a few years ago. Most require a three-night minimum stay.

If you like to get out and explore, you may prefer an EP property. Many places offer MAP or FAP packages that include such extras as airport transfers and tours. Even if you don't want to be tied down to a meal plan, it pays to inquire, because the savings can be considerable. Rooms at most hotels are equipped with cable or satellite TV, air-conditioning, direct-dial phone, clock radio, and, in many cases, a safe. Larger properties usually have no-smoking rooms and rooms accessible to travelers with disabilities, as well as room service, laundry service, meeting rooms and business services, shops, a beauty parlor, a tour desk, and car rentals.

Jamaica's resorts and hotels have varying policies about children; some don't accept children under 16 or 18 years old, but those that do often allow up to two to stay free in their parents' room. Others allow kids to stay free in the off-season, or offer discounted meal plans. Baby-sitting is readily available at properties that accept children. If you plan to bring the kids, ask lots of questions before making a reservation, or have your travel agent find the best deal.

Please note that the price categories listed below are based on winter rates. As a rule, rates are reduced anywhere from 10% to 30% from April 30 to December 15. All price categories are assigned based on standard double rooms at the most comprehensive (and most expensive) meal-plan rate. Opting for a less comprehensive plan (if it's available in winter) can save you 20%–40%. The **Jamaica reservations service** (☎ 800/526–2422 in the U.S. and Canada) can book resorts, hotels, villas, and guest houses throughout the country.

CATEGORY	COST EP/CP*	COST MAP**	COST AI***
$$$$	over $245	over $250	over $275
$$$	$175–$245	$190–$250	$225–$275
$$	$105–$175	$130–$190	$175–$225
$	under $105	under $130	under $175

EP prices are for a standard double room for two in winter, excluding 10% tax and any service charge. Many hotels either include breakfast in the tariff or offer a CP price, which includes breakfast as their minimum plan.

**MAP prices include daily breakfast and dinner for two in winter. Often MAP packages come with use of nonmotorized water sports and other benefits.*

***All-inclusive (AI) winter prices are per person, double occupancy, and include tax, service, gratuities, all meals, drinks, facilities, lessons, and airport transfers. Motorized water sports and scuba are sometimes included; if it's important to you, ask.*

Kingston

Some of the island's finest business hotels are in Kingston, and those high towers are filled with rooftop restaurants, English pubs, serious theater and pantomime, dance presentations, art museums and galleries, jazz clubs, upscale supper clubs, and disco dives.

$$$$ ⊡ **Strawberry Hill.** One of many island properties owned
★ by Chris Blackwell, formerly the head of Island Records (the late Bob Marley's label), this Blue Mountains retreat 45 min-

utes north of Kingston offers refined luxury and absolute peace. Authors, musicians, and screenwriters come here for extended periods to relax, rejuvenate the creative juices, and work. The food is top notch, as are the staff and the accommodations—elegant Georgian-style villas with mahogany furnishings and roomy balconies that have grand vistas. There's no air-conditioning here, simply because it's not needed at 3,100 ft above sea level. Sunday brunch, with an enormous Jamaican buffet, is an affair to remember, but reserve a spot early—it's a favored event among Kingston's movers and shakers. The resort recently added an Aveda spa with a full line of treatments. ✉ *New Castle Rd., Irishtown, St. Andrew,* ☎ *876/944–8400 or 800/688–7678 (reservations service),* FAX *876/944–8408. 12 1-, 2-, and 3-bedroom villas. Restaurant, bar, refrigerators, room service, sauna, spa, croquet, airport shuttle. AE, MC, V. CP.*

$$$ 🏨 **Crowne Plaza Kingston.** This ocher-color high-rise sits on a hill in Constant Spring, a classy Kingston suburb. Sophisticated public areas are adorned with potted plants, overstuffed furniture, and intriguing Jamaican art. Decor varies from floor to floor; some of the amenity-laden rooms are blue-on-white, while others feature burgundy, yellow, and green color schemes and a mix of florals and plaids. There are business-class rooms that have in-room faxes and modems among their extra amenities. Request a room on the southwest side for grand sunset views, or time your dinner at Isabella's, the hotel's fine dining room, to catch the dwindling rays. ✉ *211A Constant Spring Rd.,* ☎ *876/ 925–7676 or 800/618–6534 (reservations service),* FAX *876/925–5757. 115 rooms, 40 suites. Restaurant, 2 bars, grill, in-room safes, kitchenettes, minibars, refrigerators, room service, pool, massage, sauna, tennis court, exercise room, jogging, squash, concierge. AE, DC, MC, V. EP.*

$$$ 🏨 **Le Méridien Pegasus.** This 17-story complex near downtown has an efficient and accommodating staff, Old World decor, and a newly renovated lobby. Other features here include an excellent business center, duty-free shops, and 24-hour room service. Guests on the business floors can check out complimentary cellular phones for use during their stay. At press time, only three floors (9–11) of rooms—all with balcony, coffee/tea setups, and voice mail—had received desperately needed face-lifts. ✉ *81 Knutsford Blvd. (Box*

Jamaica Lodging

Astra Country Inn & Restaurant, **43**

Bonnie View Plantation Hotel, **31**

Boscobel Beach, **26**

Breezes Golf and Beach Resort, **14**

Charela Inn, **48**

Ciboney, Ocho Rios, **27**

Club Caribbean, **15**

Club Jamaica Beach Resort, **22**

Coco La Palm, **50**

Comfort Suites, **19**

Couples, **25**

Crowne Plaza Kingston, **40**

Dragon Bay, **30**

Enchanted Garden, **20**

FDR, Franklyn D. Resort, **16**

Goblin Hill, **35**

Grand Lido Braco Village Resort, **53**

Grand Lido Negril, **55**

Grand Lido San Souci, **28**

Hedonism II, **52**

Hibiscus Lodge, **23**

High Hope Estate, **18**

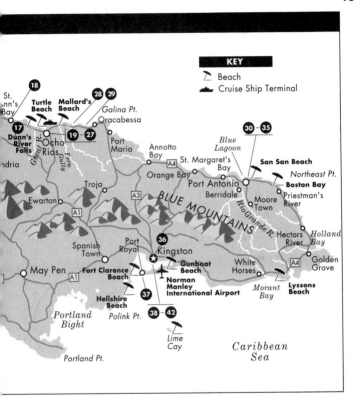

KEY

⌇ Beach

⛴ Cruise Ship Terminal

Hotel Mocking Bird Hill, **34**
Jamaica Inn, **29**
Jamaica Palace, **33**
Jonreine Country Inn, **41**
Le Méridien Pegasus, **42**
Mandeville Hotel, **44**

Morgan's Harbour Hotel, Beach Club, and Yacht Marina, **37**
Negril Cabins Resort, **54**
Negril Gardens, **47**
Plantation Inn, **24**
Point Village, **45**

Renaissance Jamaica Grande, **21**
Rockhouse, **46**
Sandals Dunn's River Golf Resort and Spa, **17**
Sandals Negril Beach Resort and Spa, **51**

Strawberry Hill, **36**
Swept Away, **49**
Terra Nova, **39**
Trident Villas and Hotel, **32**
Wyndham New Kingston, **38**

333), ☎ 876/926–3690 or 800/225–5843 *(reservations service)*, ℻ 876/929–5855. *325 rooms, 16 suites. 2 restaurants, 2 bars, coffee shop, in-room safes, minibars, room service, pool, wading pool, beauty salon, 2 tennis courts, basketball, exercise room, jogging, shops, playground, concierge, business services. AE, DC, MC, V. EP, MAP.*

$$–$$$ 🏨 **Wyndham New Kingston.** This high-rise Wyndham is the best of Kingston's business hotels. The expansive marble lobby leads to attractive, well-appointed guest rooms. The concierge floors include complimentary cocktails, hors d'oeuvres, and Continental breakfast. There are lots of extras throughout: secured-access elevators, an American Airlines service desk, and in-room coffee/tea setups. Rates include admission to Jonkanoo, the hotel's hot nightclub (☞ Chapter 6); there's also an art gallery. A meal at the Palm Court (☞ Chapter 3), will surely make your day (or night). ⊠ *75 Knutsford Blvd. (Box 112),* ☎ *876/926–5430 or 800/526–2422 (reservations service),* ℻ *876/929–7439. 284 rooms, 13 suites, 6 1- and 2-bedroom units. 2 restaurants, 3 bars, in-room modem lines, in-room safes, pool, massage, sauna, 2 tennis courts, health club, shops, recreation room, concierge. AE, DC, MC, V. EP, MAP.*

$$ 🏨 **Morgan's Harbour Hotel, Beach Club, and Yacht Marina.** A favorite of the sail-into-Jamaica set, this small property has 22 acres of beachfront at the very entrance to the old pirate's town. Done in light tropical prints, the rooms are very basic, but many have a balcony and a mini-refrigerator; the suites with loft bedrooms are the nicest. Ask for one in the newer wing. Because the hotel is so close to the airport, passengers on delayed or canceled flights are often bused here to wait. ⊠ *Port Royal,* ☎ *876/967–8040,* ℻ *876/967–8073. 44 rooms, 6 suites. Restaurant, bar, room service, pool, volleyball, dive shop, snorkeling, boating, fishing, billiards, dance club, airport shuttle. AE, MC, V. EP.*

$$ 🏨 **Terra Nova.** Set in the quieter part of New Kingston, 1 mi from the commercial district and within walking distance of Devon House, a historic home surrounded by boutiques and fine restaurants, is this intimate hotel. Guest rooms are decked out in classical mahogany furniture and fine art. The El Dorado restaurant offers international cuisine and reasonably priced buffets. You'll also find formal high-tea service here on Thursday. ⊠ *17 Waterloo Rd.,* ☎

876/926–9334, FAX *876/929–4933. 35 rooms. Restaurant, coffee shop, grill, in-room safes, no-smoking rooms, room service, pool. AE, DC, MC, V. EP.*

$ ☷ **Jonreine Country Inn.** High above Kingston, this small inn commands a view of the city, the sea, and the mountains. Once a private home, the former bedrooms have been converted into spacious guest quarters, each with private bath. The Forbidden Heights restaurant serves Chinese specialties and seafood and is a top place to see and be seen in Kingston. In the late hours, the owners take guests out for Kingston nightlife. ⊠ *7 West Kirkland Heights, Forest Hills,* ☎ *876/944–3340, 876/944–3513, or 800/526–2422 (reservations service);* FAX *876/944–3513. 14 rooms. Restaurant, bar, baby-sitting. AE, DC, MC, V. CP.*

Mandeville

At 2,000 ft above the sea, Mandeville is noted for its cool climate and proximity to secluded south-coast beaches. Most accommodations don't have air-conditioning (you really don't need it). Many are close to golf, tennis, horseback riding, and bird-watching areas.

$ ☷ **Astra Country Inn & Restaurant.** "Country" is the key word in the name of this retreat, which is 2,000 ft up in the mountains. The low price reflects the nature of the very basic rooms here: they're spartan but immaculately clean. The small restaurant is open from 7 AM to 9 PM and serves snacks in addition to breakfast, lunch, and dinner. The food is billed as "home cooking" and emphasizes fresh produce—lots of vegetables and fruit juices. The tariff here includes breakfast. ⊠ *62 Ward Ave. (Box 60),* ☎ *876/962–7979 or 876/962–3725,* FAX *876/962–1461. 20 rooms, 1 suite. Restaurant, bar, kitchenettes, pool, sauna, laundry service. AE, MC, V. CP.*

$ ☷ **Mandeville Hotel.** Tropical gardens wrap around the building, and flowers spill onto the terrace restaurant, where breakfast and lunch are served. Rooms are simple and breeze-cooled; suites have full kitchens. You'll need a car to get around town, go out for dinner, and get to the beach, which is an hour away. ⊠ *4 Hotel St. (Box 78),* ☎ *876/962–2460,* FAX *876/962–0700. 46 rooms, 17 1-, 2-,* *and 3-bedroom suites. Restaurant, bar, coffee shop, re-frigerators, pool, golf privileges, baby-sitting, laundry ser-vice, meeting room, travel services. AE, MC, V. EP.*

Montego Bay

MoBay (as it's affectionately called) has miles of hotels, vil-las, apartments, and duty-free shops. Although lacking much in the way of cultural stimuli, it presents a comfort-able island backdrop for the many conventions it hosts.

$$$$ 🏨 **Half Moon Golf, Tennis, and Beach Club.** For more than
★   40 years this 400-acre resort has been a destination unto itself, with a reputation for doing the little things right. Al-though it has mushroomed from 30 to more than 400 units, it has maintained an intimate, luxurious feel. The rooms, suites, and villas—whether done in a modern or a Queen Anne style—are exquisitely decorated with such flourishes as Asian rugs and antique radios. Several villas (which come with a cook, a butler, a housekeeper, and a rental car or golf cart) have private pools, and the mile-long stretch of beach is just steps away from every room. On the grounds there's an upscale shopping mall as well as a nature reserve and a hospital. The Sugar Mill restaurant (☞ Chapter 3) is sure to serve something that will please you. ⊠ *7 mi east of MoBay (Box 80),* ☎ *876/953–2211 or 800/237–3237 (reservations service),* ⅎ⅍ *876/953–2731. 417 units. 7 restaurants, 3 bars, 2 pools, outdoor hot tub, sauna, spa, 18-hole golf course, 13 tennis courts, aerobics, badminton, croquet, exercise room, horseback riding, Ping-Pong, squash, beach, dive shop, snorkeling, windsurfing, bicycles, shops, theater, library, children's programs, play-ground, convention center. AE, DC, MC, V. All-inclusive, EP, FAP, MAP.*

$$$$ 🏨 **Round Hill Hotel and Villas.** The Hollywood set frequents
★   this peaceful resort, 8 mi west of town on a hilly peninsula. Twenty-seven villas with 74 suites are set on 98 acres, and there are 36 hotel rooms in Pineapple House, a building that overlooks the sea. Rooms are done in a refined Ralph Lau-ren style, with mahogany furnishings and terra-cotta floors. The villas are leased back to the resort by private owners and vary in decor, but jungle motifs are a favorite. All come with a personal maid and a cook (for an extra charge) to

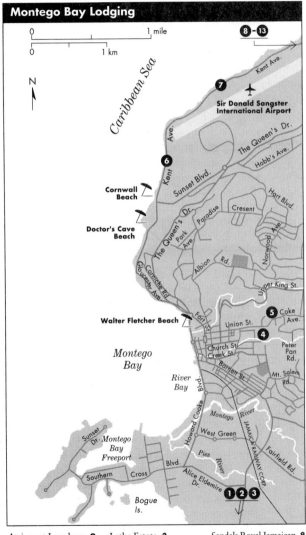

Montego Bay Lodging

Atrium at Ironshore, **9**
Coyaba Beach Resort and Club, **10**
Half Moon Golf, Tennis, and Beach Club, **11**
Holiday Inn Sunspree Resort, **12**
Lethe Estate, **3**
Richmond Hill Inn, **5**
Round Hill Hotel and Villas, **2**
Sandals Inn, **6**
Sandals Montego Bay, **7**
Sandals Royal Jamaican, **8**
Tryall Golf, Tennis, and Beach Club, **1**
Verney's Tropical Resort, **4**
Wyndham Rose Hall, **13**

make your breakfast, and several have private pools. The restaurant's good food and elegant presentation make a meal in the dining room, or better yet on the seaside terrace, memorable. ✉ *8 mi west of Montego Bay on North Coast Hwy. (Box 64),* ☎ *876/956–7050 or 800/237–3237 (reservations service),* ℻ *876/956–7505. 36 rooms, 27 villas. Restaurant, room service, pool, beauty salon, massage, 5 tennis courts, aerobics, exercise room, jogging, beach, dive shop, snorkeling, windsurfing, shops, concierge, helipad. AE, DC, MC, V. All-inclusive, EP, FAP, MAP.*

$$$$ ⛳ **Tryall Golf, Tennis, and Beach Club.** Part of a posh residential development 15 mi west of MoBay, Tryall clings to a hilltop that overlooks a golf course and the Caribbean. Here you'll stay in one of the numerous villas—each with its own pool, full staff (butler, cook, maid, and gardener), and golf cart—that dot the 2,200-acre island plantation. All accommodations are individually and plushly decorated. The fine dining room in the great house is elegant and serves Continental and Jamaican cuisine. The beautiful seaside golf course is one of this resort's more memorable features. It's also reputed to be one of the meanest courses in the world, and, as such, hosts big-money tournaments. ✉ *15 mi west of MoBay on North Coast Hwy. (Box 1206),* ☎ *876/956–5660, 876/956–5667, or 800/238–5290 (reservations service);* ℻ *876/956–5658. 57 villas. Restaurant, 4 bars, refrigerators, pool, massage, driving range, 18-hole golf course, 9 tennis courts, jogging, beach, dive shop, snorkeling, windsurfing. AE, DC, MC, V. EP.*

$$$–
$$$$
★ ⛳ **Coyaba Beach Resort and Club.** Owners Joanne and Kevin Robertson live on the property, interacting with guests daily and giving this oceanfront retreat the feel of an intimate and inviting country inn. Coyaba is also very family friendly. The plantation-style great house, just east of Montego Bay, successfully blends modern amenities with Old World grace. Rooms are decorated with lovely colonial prints and hand-carved mahogany furniture, and sunshine pours through the tall windows and over terracotta floors and potted plants. Part of the package is a basket with bottled springwater and freshly baked banana bread greeting you upon check-in; weekly afternoon tea and evening cocktail parties; and tennis, scuba diving, and massage. ✉ *Mahoe Bay, Little River,* ☎ *876/953–9150 or*

800/237–3237 (reservations service), FAX 876/953–2244. 50 rooms. 2 restaurants, 3 bars, pool, outdoor hot tub, massage, tennis court, exercise room, volleyball, beach, dive shop, snorkeling, windsurfing, recreation room, library, playground. AE, MC, V. All-inclusive, EP, MAP.

$$$–
$$$$ ☷ **Sandals Montego Bay.** The largest private beach in MoBay is the spark that lights this Sandals—one of the most popular couples resorts in the Caribbean. Its all-inclusive rate and nonstop activities (not to mention its rooms overlooking the bay) make it a bit like a cruise ship that remains in port. The atmosphere here is one of a great big party, despite the planes that zoom overhead (the airport is nearby). Even staff members seem happy as they hum or sing their way through the workday. Rooms are basic but comfortable enough, and you're seldom in them because there's so much to do. The Oleandor Restaurant is probably the best fine-dining establishment in the Sandals chain. ✉ Kent Ave. (Box 100), ☎ 876/952–5510 or 800/726–3257 (reservations service), FAX 876/952–0816. 246 rooms. 4 restaurants, 4 bars, snack bar, in-room safes, 4 pools, 3 outdoor hot tubs, sauna, 3 tennis courts, racquetball, beach, dive shop, dock, snorkeling, windsurfing, boating, library, concierge. 2-night minimum stay. AE, MC, V. All-inclusive.

$$$–
$$$$
★ ☷ **Sandals Royal Jamaican.** Another all-inclusive resort for couples only, this Sandals establishment is distinguished by Jamaican-style buildings that are arranged in a semicircle around attractive gardens. Although there are plenty of activities here, this resort is quieter and more genteel than Sandals Montego Bay (☞ above) and draws something of an international crowd. Deluxe rooms have mahogany four-poster beds and mauve carpeting and bedspreads; bathrooms are small. Oceanfront rooms and suites are more elegant and inviting, with mahogany four-poster beds and floral-print fabrics. A colorful "dragon boat" transports you to Sandals's private island for meals at the Indonesian restaurant. ✉ 4 mi east of airport on North Coast Hwy. (Box 167), ☎ 876/953–2231 or 800/726–3257 (reservations service), FAX 876/953–2788. 190 rooms. 4 restaurants, 4 bars, in-room safes, 4 pools, beauty salon, 5 outdoor hot tubs, sauna, 3 tennis courts, aerobics, beach, dive shop, snorkeling, windsurfing, concierge. 3-night minimum stay. AE, MC, V. All-inclusive.

$$$ 🏨 **Lethe Estate.** This quiet mountainside inn is a far cry from the bustling beach resorts for which MoBay is known. Tucked on the banks of the Great River near the village of Lethe, interruptions at this small property come not from reggae music or dance contests, but from the sounds of birds. You don't have the sea nearby, but you can take a dip in the river (or float down it on a bamboo raft), take a jitney through the nearby Lethe Estate plantation, or fish in freshwater ponds. ✉ *Reading Rd., 20 minutes west of MoBay (Box 23),* ☎ *876/956–4920,* ℻ *876/956–4927. 15 rooms. Restaurant, pool, tennis court, horseback riding, fishing, airport shuttle. AE, MC, V. CP.*

$$–$$$ 🏨 **Wyndham Rose Hall.** This self-contained resort, on the 400-acre Rose Hall Plantation, is a bustling business hotel (popular with large groups) with all the usual amenities: tennis courts, golf course, three interconnected pools, a nightclub, a water-sports center, and a shopping arcade. Rooms, which were renovated in 1997, are done in tropical florals in shades of deep peach and are comfortable, though somewhat sterile. The waters off the thin crescent beach are good for sailing and snorkeling. ✉ *4 mi east of airport on North Coast Hwy. (Box 999),* ☎ *876/953–2650 or 800/996–3426 (reservations service),* ℻ *876/953–2617. 470 rooms, 19 suites. 4 restaurants, 3 bars, in-room safes, room service, 3 pools, massage, 6 tennis courts, 18-hole golf course, aerobics, basketball, exercise room, volleyball, beach, dive shop, snorkeling, windsurfing, nightclub, children's program, playground, convention center. AE, DC, MC, V. All-inclusive, EP, MAP.*

$$ 🏨 **Sandals Inn.** If you can forego a private beach (there's a public one across the street), you can stay here for much less than at other couples-only Sandals operations. Managed more as a small hotel than a large resort, this establishment is intimate and relatively quiet. The charming rooms are compact; most have balconies that face the pool. Dark carpet contrasts with white lacquered furniture and tropical-print fabrics. There's plenty to do here, and you can get in on the action at the other two MoBay Sandals by hopping on the free hourly shuttle. The in-town location puts you close to shops and sights. ✉ *Gloucester Ave. (Box 412),* ☎ *876/952–4140 or 800/726–3257 (reservations service),* ℻ *876/952–6913. 52 rooms. 2 restaurants,*

2 bars, in-room safes, pool, beauty salon, outdoor hot tub, tennis court, concierge, airport shuttle. 3-night minimum stay. AE, MC, V. All-inclusive.

$–$$ ⛨ **Atrium at Ironshore.** Fifteen moderately priced, fully furnished apartments make up this small complex. Decor varies, but each unit has pastel floral and plaid prints, cool white-tile floors, rattan furniture, a patio or a balcony, and a private housekeeper-cook on call. Large saltwater tanks full of tropical fish brighten the alfresco dining terrace near the waterfall-fed pool, and you'll often find lively games of darts or skittles under way in the English-style pub. A shopping mall with a supermarket, a cinema, and several boutiques is within walking distance, but you'll have to take a shuttle to the beach. ✉ *1084 Morgan Rd. (Box 604),* ☎ *876/953–2605,* FAX *876/953–3683. 15 1½-, 2-, and 3-bedroom suites. Restaurant, pub, kitchenettes, refrigerators, pool, meeting room. AE, DC, MC, V. EP.*

$ ⛨ **Holiday Inn Sunspree Resort.** At this family-oriented resort, you'll find activities day and night. Although the rooms—spread out in seven buildings—are cheerful enough, the hotel is big and noisy (rooms farthest from the pool and central dining-entertainment area are the quietest). Room service is available for breakfast. The beach is just a palm-shaded sliver. ✉ *6 mi east of airport on North Coast Hwy. (Box 480),* ☎ *876/953–2485 or 800/352–0731 (reservations service),* FAX *876/953–2840. 496 rooms, 24 suites. 2 restaurants, 4 bars, 2 snack bars, in-room safes, no-smoking rooms, room service, pool, 4 tennis courts, beach, dive shop, snorkeling, windsurfing, children's program, playground, concierge, airport shuttle. AE, DC, MC, V. All-inclusive, EP.*

$ ⛨ **Richmond Hill Inn.** This hilltop inn—a quaint, 200-year-old great house originally owned by the Dewars clan—has spectacular views of the Caribbean and a great deal of peace. Decor tends toward the dainty: frilly lace curtains and doilies, lots of lavenders and mauves, and crushed-velvet furniture here and there. A free shuttle will take you to shops and beaches, about 10–15 minutes away. ✉ *Union St. (Box 362),* ☎ *876/952–3859 or 800/423–4095 (reservations service). 15 rooms, 5 suites. Bar, coffee shop, dining room, pool, laundry service. AE, MC, V. EP, FAP, MAP.*

$ ⛨ **Verney's Tropical Resort.** Here you'll find a terrific view of MoBay and the sea as well as a warm atmosphere. Owners Kathleen and Earnest Sterling greet you like family (they have many repeat guests). Rooms are simple but clean. You can take the free weekday shuttle down to Doctor's Cave Beach or stay on the property for a dip in the hillside pool followed by a genuine Jamaican-style meal. Tennis courts and in-town shopping areas are within walking distance. ⊠ *3 Leader Ave.,* ☎ *876/952–2875 or 876/952– 8628,* ℻ *876/979–2944. 27 rooms. Restaurant, bar, pool, baby-sitting. AE, MC, V. CP.*

Negril

Some 50 mi west of Montego Bay, Negril was long a sleepy bohemian retreat. In the last decade the town has blossomed and added a number of classy all-inclusive resorts, with several more on the drawing board for Bloody Bay (northeast of Seven Mile Beach). Negril itself is only a small village with little of historic significance. But such sights are not what draws the sybaritic singles and couples. The young, hip crowd here comes for sun, sand, and sea.

$$$$ ⊞ **Grand Lido Negril.** The dramatic entrance of marble floors
★   and columns, filled with Jamaican artwork, sets an elegant tone at this SuperClubs all-inclusive property. It's geared to folks with some money in their pockets, and it attracts mature, settled couples and singles. The well-appointed, split-level oceanfront and garden rooms are spacious and stylish. For some guests, the pièce de résistance is a sunset cruise on the resort's 147-ft yacht, *Zien,* which was a wedding gift from Aristotle Onassis to Prince Rainier and Princess Grace of Monaco. The Piacere restaurant is superb. (Note that weddings at this resort are complimentary.) ⊠ *Norman Manley Blvd. (Box 88),* ☎ *876/957–5011 or 800/467– 8737 (reservations service),* ℻ *876/957–5517. 216 rooms, 16 suites. 3 restaurants, 9 bars, in-room safes, room service, 2 pools, 2 outdoor hot tubs, massage, 4 tennis courts, beach, dive shop, snorkeling, windsurfing, library, concierge, laundry service. 3-night minimum stay. AE, DC, MC, V. All-inclusive.*

$$$–   ⊞ **Sandals Negril Beach Resort and Spa.** Couples looking
$$$$ for an upscale, sports-oriented getaway and a casual atmosphere (you can wear dressy shorts to dinner) flock to

this resort on one of the best (and longest stretches) of Negril's 7-mi beach. Water sports, particularly scuba diving, are emphasized; the capable staff is happy to work with neophytes (one pool is designated for scuba training) as well as certified veterans. There's a nearby island, a huge swim-up pool bar, and a range of spacious accommodations. Both rooms and staff are sunny and appealing. ⊠ *Norman Manley Blvd. (Box 12),* ☎ *876/957–5216 or 800/726–3257 (reservations service),* ℻ *876/957–5338. 215 rooms. 4 restaurants, 4 bars, in-room safes, 3 pools, 2 outdoor hot tubs, saunas, 4 tennis courts, racquetball, squash, beach, dive shop, snorkeling, windsurfing, concierge. 3-night minimum stay. AE, MC, V. All-inclusive.*

$$$– $$$$ ★ 🏨 **Swept Away.** With its emphasis on sports and healthful cuisine, it's no wonder that this resort attracts fitness-minded couples. The suites are in 26 cottages—each with a private garden atrium—that are spread out along a ½-mi stretch of gorgeous beach. There's an outstanding 10-acre sports complex across the road. At the Feathers Continental restaurant (open to nonguests), the chefs prepare dishes designed to keep you fit and trim with lots of fish, white meat, and fresh fruits and vegetables. Complimentary weddings are part of the all-inclusive package. ⊠ *Norman Manley Blvd., Long Bay,* ☎ *876/957–4061 or 800/ 545–7937 (reservations service),* ℻ *876/957–4060. 134 suites. 2 restaurants, 4 bars, in-room safes, pool, 2 outdoor hot tubs, massage, 2 saunas, spa, 2 steam rooms, 10 tennis courts, aerobics, health club, jogging, racquetball, squash, beach, dive shop, snorkeling, windsurfing. 3-night minimum stay. AE, DC, MC, V. All-inclusive.*

$$$ 🏨 **Point Village.** This moderately priced resort is family friendly. Rooms have tile floors and basic furnishings, and each is decorated according to its owner's taste. Highly popular with tour groups, this sprawling property has two small crescent beaches, rocky grottoes to explore, fine snorkeling just offshore, and a petting zoo. If you don't opt for the all-inclusive plan, the one- and two-bedroom housekeeping suites with kitchens are a good choice. ⊠ *Norman Manley Blvd. (Box 105),* ☎ *876/957–5170 or 800/752– 6824 (reservations service),* ℻ *876/957–5351. 177 units. Restaurant, 3 bars, 2 grills, grocery, fresh- and saltwater pools, outdoor hot tub, massage, tennis court, aerobics,*

beach, snorkeling, windsurfing, children's programs, playground. AE, MC, V. All-inclusive, EP, FAP, MAP.

$$–$$$ 🎬 **Negril Cabins Resort.** These elevated, timber cottages are nestled amid lush vegetation and towering royal palms. Rooms are open and airy, with floral bedspreads, gauzy curtains, natural wood floors, and high ceilings. The most popular rooms have TVs and air-conditioning; others have no TV and are cooled by ceiling fans and breezes that come through slatted windows. The gleaming beach across the road is filled with sunbathers and water-sports enthusiasts; for shopping, you can take the shuttle into town. A most convivial place, this property is popular with young Europeans. Reasonably priced dive packages are available, and children under 12 stay free in their parents' room. ✉ *Norman Manley Blvd. (Box 118),* ☎ *876/957–5350 or 800/382–3444 (reservations service),* ℻ *876/957–5381. 80 rooms, 2 suites. 3 restaurants, 3 bars, in-room safes, room service, pool, outdoor hot tub, tennis court, exercise room, beach, dive shop, snorkeling, recreation room, baby-sitting, playground. AE, MC, V. EP, MAP.*

$–$$$ 🎬 **Hedonism II.** Hedonism appeals mostly to single (60% of guests are), uninhibited vacationers age 18 and over who like a robust mix of physical activities. (You can try everything from scuba diving to a trampoline clinic.) Public areas are filled with potted plants and scantily clad guests. Handsome guest rooms have modern blond-wood furniture and mirrored ceilings above king-size or twin beds. There's no TV, but phones were added in 1997, as were a skinny-dipping pool and hot tub. Wooden floors in the open-air halls tend to amplify the noise. Solo guests pay a hefty supplement or are assigned a roommate of the same sex. With both "nude" and "prude" beaches, the atmosphere here is lively around the clock. Most guests prefer the nude beach, with its new pool and swim-up bar. Scheduled activities include nude body painting, volleyball—even shuffleboard in the buff. ✉ *Norman Manley Blvd. (Box 25),* ☎ *876/957–5200 or 800/859–7873 (reservations service),* ℻ *876/957–5289. 280 rooms. 2 restaurants, 6 bars, 2 grills, in-room safes, 2 pools, 2 outdoor hot tubs, 6 tennis courts, squash, beach, dive shop, snorkeling, windsurfing, boating. 3-night minimum stay. AE, DC, MC, V. All-inclusive.*

$–$$$ ⊞ **Negril Gardens.** Towering palms and well-tended gardens surround the pink and white buildings of this hotel. Half the rooms are on the beach, half (across the street) overlook the pool; all are attractive, with tile floors and rattan furniture. Water sports are available at the beach. On-site you'll find an ice cream parlor and a jerk center (for takeout). ⊠ *Norman Manley Blvd. (Box 58),* ☎ *876/957–4408 or 800/752–6824 (reservations service),* FAX *876/957–4374. 66 rooms. 2 restaurants, ice cream parlor, 2 bars, in-room safes, pool, tennis court, exercise room, beach, snorkeling. AE, MC, V. All-inclusive, CP, EP, FAP, MAP.*

$$ ⊞ **Charela Inn.** Each quiet, elegantly appointed room here has a private balcony or a covered patio. The owners' French-Jamaican roots find daily expression in La Vendome restaurant, where you can dine on local produce and seafood dressed up with French sauces; there's also an excellent selection of wines. The small beach is part of the glorious 7-mi Negril crescent. On Saturday night, many guests staying at other resorts come here to watch a folkloric show. ⊠ *Norman Manley Blvd. (Box 33),* ☎ *876/957–4277,* FAX *876/957–4414. 49 rooms. Restaurant, bar, pool, beach, windsurfing, boating, laundry service. 5-night minimum stay in high season, 3-night minimum stay in summer. MC, V. EP, MAP.*

$$ ⊞ **Coco La Palm.** This quiet seaside hotel features oversize rooms (junior suites average 525 square ft) in octagonal buildings set in a U-shape around the pool. Amenities include mini-refrigerators, coffeemakers, air-conditioning, ceiling fans, and private patios or terraces—most overlooking gardens (only seven rooms have ocean views). Centered on Negril Beach, the sandy shoreline of Coco La Palm is dotted with palm trees. The beachside restaurant is open-air and casual. ⊠ *Norman Manley Blvd.,* ☎ *876/ 957–4227 or 800/896–0987 (reservations service),* FAX *876/957–3460. 41 rooms. Restaurant, bar, grill, air-conditioning, fans, refrigerators, pool, outdoor hot tub, beach. AE, DC, MC, V. EP, MAP.*

$–$$ ⊞ **Rockhouse.** You're side by side with nature at this stylish resort on Negril's rugged cliffs. Accommodations are built from rough-hewn timber, thatch, and stone and are filled with furniture that echoes the nature theme. All rooms have private, indoor baths, but even these seem rustic; villa rooms have private, enclosed, outdoor showers. There's a thatched-roof Jamaican restaurant and a cliff-top pool and bar. At press time, the resort was adding eight studio units to its west side. Owing to the steep cliffs, parents traveling with children under 12 are well advised to rule out a stay here. ⊠ *West End Rd. (Box 24),* ☎ *876/957–4373,* FAX *876/957–4373. 20 rooms. Restaurant, 2 bars, in-room safes, minibars, pool, snorkeling. AE, MC, V. EP.*

Ocho Rios

On the northeast coast halfway between Port Antonio and Montego Bay, Ocho Rios is hilly and lush. Its resorts (many all-inclusive), hotels, and villas are all a short drive from a bustling crafts market; boutiques and duty-free shops; restaurants; and several scenic attractions.

$$$$ 🏨 **Boscobel Beach.** Families are made to feel very welcome
★ at this all-inclusive resort. Everybody is kept busy all week for a single package price, and everyone leaves happy. The cheery day-care centers group children by age and offer an array of entertaining and educational activities. Thoughtfully, there's an adults-only section of the resort (for when the kids want to get away—perhaps to the petting zoo). Bedspreads in bright sea-life motifs or soothing pastel florals spice up the white tile floors and creamy walls of the rooms and suites. Like other members of the SuperClubs family, this resort offers free weddings. ⊠ *Boscobel, St. Mary (Box 63),* ☎ *876/975–7330 or 800/467–8737 (reservations service),* FAX *876/975–7370. 64 rooms, 152 junior suites. 5 restaurants, 5 bars, in-room safes, refrigerators, 2 pools, wading pool, 2 outdoor hot tubs, massage, 4 tennis courts, beach, children's programs, nursery, playground. 3-night minimum stay. AE, DC, MC, V. All-inclusive.*

$$$$ 🏨 **Ciboney, Ocho Rios.** This stately plantation property has 56 rooms in its great house and 226 spacious one-, two-, and three-bedroom villa suites on 45 lush hillside acres. It's run by Radisson as an upscale, all-inclusive for singles and couples. Outstanding features are the European-style spa (you receive a complimentary massage, manicure, and pedicure) and four signature restaurants, including the Orchids, whose menu was developed by the Culinary Institute of America. Every villa has an attendant and a pool, for the ultimate in privacy and pampering. The decor is casual and contemporary—light-color rattan furnishings, tile floors, and pastel fabrics. If there are drawbacks here, it's how busy the place is and the fact that the private beach is a shuttle ride away. ⊠ *104 Main St. (Box 728),* ☎ *876/ 974–1027 or 800/333–3333 (reservations service),* FAX *876/974–7148. 226 1-, 2-, and 3-bedroom suites, 56 rooms. 4 restaurants, 6 bars, in-room safes, kitchenettes, minibars, refrigerators, in-room VCRs, 2 pools, 1 indoor and 5 outdoor hot tubs, 2 saunas, spa, 2 steam rooms, 6 tennis courts, aerobics, basketball, croquet, squash, beach, dive shop, snorkeling, windsurfing, dance club, concierge. AE, DC, MC, V. All-inclusive.*

$$$$
★ **Grand Lido Sans Souci.** This pastel-pink cliffside resort looks and feels like a fantasy. A stay here is a wonderfully luxurious experience. Romantic oceanfront suites are equipped with oversize whirlpool tubs. Blond-wood furniture, cool tile floors, and sheer curtains are accented by pastel watercolors and Jamaican prints on the walls. A highlight is the pampering you receive at Charlie's Spa in the form of a massage, body scrub, reflexology session, facial, manicure, and even a complimentary manicure and pedicure (book treatments as soon as you arrive, if not before). Complimentary weddings are part of the all-inclusive package. ⊠ *2 mi east of Ocho Rios (Box 103),* ☎ *876/974– 2353 or 800/467–8737 (reservations service),* FAX *876/ 974–2544. 13 rooms, 98 suites. 3 restaurants, 4 bars, grill, in-room safes, minibars, 2 pools, hot tub, massage, spa, 4 tennis courts, beach, library, laundry service, concierge. 3- night minimum stay. AE, D, DC, MC, V. All-inclusive.*

$$$$
⊞ **Jamaica Inn.** A combination of class and quiet attracts a discerning crowd to this vintage property. Each room has its own veranda (larger than most hotel rooms) on the private cove's powdery champagne-color beach. The colonial decor is on the dark side, with Jamaican antique furniture, terrazzo floors, and walls hung with oil paintings (there are no TVs or radios). Jacket and tie are de rigueur after 7 PM during high season (December–April). ⊠ *East of Ocho Rios on North Coast Hwy. (Box 1),* ☎ *876/974–2514 or 800/ 837–4670 (reservations service),* FAX *876/974–2449. 44 rooms, 1 suite with private pool. Restaurant, 2 bars, room service, pool, croquet, exercise room, beach, snorkeling, boating, library. AE, MC, V. FAP (summer only), MAP.*

$$$$ ⊞ **Sandals Dunn's River Golf Resort and Spa.** Twenty-five
★ acres of manicured gardens surround this luxury, couples-
only all-inclusive. The pillared masterpiece, set on a wide sugary beach, is the finest of Sandals's Jamaican resorts. The
rooms are larger than at other Sandals establishments and
are decorated in light pink, blue, turquoise, and cream. Most
have a balcony or patio that overlooks the sea or the lush
grounds. Oceanfront suites have four-poster mahogany beds.
The resort draws a well-heeled crowd in their thirties and
forties, lots of honeymooners, and prides itself on catering
to every guest's every whim. A 9-hole pitch and putt is on
the grounds, and an 18-hole course is nearby. ⊠ *2 mi east
of Ocho Rios on North Coast Hwy. (Box 51),* ☎ *876/972–
1610 or 800/726–3257 (reservations service),* FAX *876/972–
1611. 256 rooms, 10 suites. 4 restaurants, 7 bars, in-room
safes, 2 pools, 3 outdoor hot tubs, sauna, spa, steam room,
putting green, 2 tennis courts, racquetball, beach, concierge.
3-night minimum stay. AE, MC, V. All-inclusive.*

$$$– ⊞ **Plantation Inn.** Looking so much like a Deep South plan-
$$$$ tation—à la *Gone With the Wind*—this inn conjures up an
existence as soft as a southern drawl. All its big, breezy rooms
have large private balconies with dramatic sea views. Cor-
ner rooms, which have mahogany half-canopy beds, are the
most romantic. Afternoon tea is served, and you can dine
by candlelight on Jamaican cuisine in the popular restau-
rant (where dancing is also an option). ⊠ *Main St. (Box 2),*
☎ *876/974–5601 or 800/752–6824 (reservations service),*
FAX *876/974–5912. 59 rooms, 17 suites. Restaurant, 2 bars,
pool, massage, sauna, 2 tennis courts, croquet, exercise
room, beach, snorkeling, windsurfing, library, children's
programs. AE, MC, V. All-inclusive, EP, MAP.*

$$–$$$$ ⊞ **Couples.** The emphasis here is on romantic (and all-in-
★ clusive) adventures for two. One-bedroom suites are designed
for romance, with two-person hot tubs in the bathroom that
peek through a window at the four-poster king-size bed.
The newer wing has 40 rooms furnished in hand-carved mahogany. There's a lovely white beach for relaxation or
water sports, and a private island where you can sunbathe
in the buff. Weddings are included in the package. ⊠ *Tower
Isle, St. Mary,* ☎ *876/975–4271 or 800/268–7537 (reservations service),* FAX *876/975–4439. 201 rooms, 11 suites.
4 restaurants, 6 bars, in-room safes, room service, pool,*

5 outdoor hot tubs, massage, sauna, 5 tennis courts, horse-back riding, squash, beach, dive shop, snorkeling, wind-surfing. 3-night minimum stay. AE, MC, V. All-inclusive.

$$$ 🏨 **High Hope Estate.** The tranquillity here is undisturbed, the vista of Caribbean coast superb. Set on 40 acres in trade-wind-cooled hills 7 mi west of Ocho Rios, this 15th-century-style villa has Italian marble floors, graceful arches, mahogany trim, and spacious verandas. The staff is warm and attentive, and owner Dennis Rapaport is a charming host who's full of fascinating stories. There are no planned activities, no disco, no bustling beach (it's 10 minutes away by car); come to enjoy the peace, to explore the hibiscus- and orchid-dotted lawns, to listen to birdsong, and to watch for shooting stars. Families and groups can book the entire villa on an all-inclusive package, but rooms are also available on a bed-and-breakfast basis. ⊠ *St. Ann's Bay (Box 11),* ☎ *876/972–2277,* ℻ *876/972–1607. 6 rooms. Fans, pool, tennis court, library, laundry service. MC, V. All-inclusive, CP, EP.*

$$–$$$ 🏨 **Enchanted Garden.** The 20 acres of gardens here, filled with tropical plants and flowers and punctuated by streams and waterfalls, are enchanting. You'll also find an aviary and a seaquarium, where you can enjoy a deli lunch or tea surrounded by tanks of fish and hanging orchids. The futuristic cream-color villas (some with private plunge pools) seem somewhat out of place amid the natural splendor, but the rooms (on the small side) are comfortable, and you're never far from the soothing sound of rushing water. Don't miss the guided garden tour, just one of dozens of activities here. There's a free shuttle to the beach, several minutes away. ⊠ *Eden Bower Rd. (Box 284),* ☎ *876/974–1400 or 800/554–2008 (reservations service),* ℻ *876/974–5823. 113 units. 5 restaurants, 4 bars, 2 pools, outdoor hot tub, sauna, spa, Turkish bath, 2 tennis courts, croquet, beach, dive shop, snorkeling, windsurfing, airport shuttle. AE, DC, MC, V. All-inclusive.*

$$ 🏨 **Renaissance Jamaica Grande.** The largest conference hotel in Jamaica attracts all types of traveler: families, couples, singles (there are special singles activities, and no singles supplement fees), and conference attendees. Even though it's a beachfront resort, the focal point is definitely the tiered and winding pool, which has a waterfall, a swaying bridge, and a swim-up bar. Rooms in the south building are the largest, but those in the north building have slightly better views. Kids are kept busy in the daily Club Mongoose activity program (included in the rates). The hotel's disco, Jamaic'N Me Crazy (☞ Chapter 6), is *very* popular. ⊠ *Main St. (Box 100),* ☎ *876/974–2201 or 800/468–3571 (reservations service),* ℻ *876/974–2289. 706 rooms, 14 suites. 5 restaurants, 9 bars, in-room safes, 3 pools, 2 outdoor hot tubs, massage, 4 tennis courts, beach, dive shop, snorkeling, windsurfing, boating, children's programs, nursery, playground, concierge, convention center. AE, DC, MC, V. All-inclusive, EP.*

$–$$ **☷ Club Jamaica Beach Resort.** At this intimate all-inclu-
★   sive you get lots of personal attention from the young, cheerful staff. Rooms are refreshing, with gleaming white-tile floors, modern furnishings, and gem-tone color schemes; more than half look out on the ocean. Guests, identified by their plastic, hospital-style bracelets, tend to be active middle-agers; most participate fully in the resort's daily activities (including nonmotorized water sports on the public beach). They also dance the night away to live music. The Ocho Rios crafts market is adjacent to the resort. ⊠ *Turtle Beach (Box 342),* ☎ *876/974–6632 or 800/818–2964 (reservations service),* ℻ *876/974–6644. 95 rooms. Restaurant, 3 bars, in-room safes, pool, outdoor hot tub, beach, dive shop, snorkeling, windsurfing, jet skiing. AE, MC, V. All-inclusive.*

$ **☷ Comfort Suites.** Families on a budget planning an extended stay should consider a suite here; the fully stocked kitchens can help keep the dining bills down. This is also one of the few places you'll find no-smoking rooms (if you want one, be sure to request it when booking). Each spacious, immaculate unit has white-tile floors, rattan furniture, and tropical floral prints. The two-bedroom suite has an open bathroom (it's divided from the main room by only a screen), as well as a whirlpool tub in its master-bedroom loft. This hotel is not on the beach (though it's close enough to walk to and a shuttle is provided), but suites in "A" block do have a partial ocean view. ⊠ *17 Da Costa Dr.,* ☎ *876/974–8050 or 800/221–2222 (reservations service),* ℻ *876/974–8070. 87 1- and 2-bedroom suites. Restaurant, bar, in-room safes, kitchenettes, no-smoking rooms, re-*

And just in case.

We're here with American Express® Travelers Cheques and Cheques *for Two.*® They're the safest way to carry money on your vacation and the surest way to get a refund, practically anywhere, anytime.
Another way we help you...

do more

AMERICAN
EXPRESS

Travelers
Cheques

frigerators, room service, outdoor hot tub, tennis court, airport shuttle. AE, DC, MC, V. EP, FAP, MAP.

$ 🏨 **Hibiscus Lodge.** This gleaming white building with a blue awning sits amid beautifully manicured lawns, not too far from a tiny private beach. The impeccably neat, cozy rooms have just about everything you need (except phones), including TVs, air-conditioning, private (shower-only) baths, and terraces with partial sea views. The place is such a bargain that many of its guests return time and time again. There are two reefs just off the beach, so the snorkeling is great here. Breakfast is included in the room rate. ✉ *83–87 Main St. (Box 52),* ☎ *876/974–2676 or 800/526–2422 (reservations service),* 🖷 *876/974–1874. 26 rooms. Restaurant, bar, air-conditioning, pool, outdoor hot tub, tennis court. AE, DC, MC, V. CP.*

Port Antonio

Described by poet Ella Wheeler Wilcox as "the most exquisite port on earth," Port Antonio is a seaside town nestled at the foot of verdant hills toward the east end of the north coast. The area's must-do activities include rafting the Rio Grande, snorkeling or scuba diving in the Blue Lagoon, exploring Nonsuch Caves, and stopping at the classy Trident resort for lunch or a drink.

$$$$ 🏨 **Trident Villas and Hotel.** The truly gracious living and
★ white-gloved dining here will transport you back to the days of the Empire. Peacocks strut the manicured lawns, colonnaded walkways wind through whimsically sculpted topiaries that dot the 14 acres, and the pool—on a rocky bit of land that juts out into crashing surf—is a memory unto itself. The luxurious Laura Ashley–style rooms—many with turrets, bay windows, and balconies or verandas—are awash in mahogany and local art; they do not have TVs or clocks. ✉ *Anchovy (Box 119),* ☎ *876/993–2602 or 800/ 428–4734 (reservations service),* 🖷 *876/993–2590. 8 rooms, 12 suites, 14 villas. Restaurant, bar, in-room safes, minibars, pool, massage, 2 tennis courts, aerobics, croquet, beach, snorkeling, boating, library, concierge. AE, MC, V. CP, FAP, MAP.*

$$$ 🏨 **Goblin Hill.** This lush 12-acre estate is set atop a hill overlooking San San Bay. Each attractively appointed villa comes with its own dramatic view, plus a staff member to do the grocery shopping, cleaning, and cooking for you. The villas are not equipped with phones or TVs, but have ceiling fans and a tropical decor. The beach is a 10-minute walk away. Excellent villa and car-rental packages are available. ⊠ *San San (Box 26),* ☎ *876/925–8108 or 800/ 472–1148 (reservations service),* ℻ *876/925–6248. 28 villas. Bar, kitchenettes, pool, 2 tennis courts, beach, dive shop, library. AE, MC, V. EP.*

$$ ⚅ **Hotel Mocking Bird Hill.** With only 10 rooms overlooking the sea and the Blue Mountains, Mocking Bird Hill feels more like a cozy B&B than a hotel. Owners Barbara Walker and Shireen Aga run an extremely environmentally sensitive operation: You'll find bamboo, instead of hardwood, furniture; solar-heated water; ceiling fans instead of ozone-depleting air-conditioning systems; meals made with local produce in the Mille Fleurs dining terrace (which is open to the public); locally produced toiletries and stationery sets; and 7 naturally landscaped acres. The tasteful blue-and-white rooms do not have phones or TVs, and most are designated no-smoking. There's also an array of eco-tour options. ⊠ *Port Antonio (Box 254) ,* ☎ *876/993–7267,* ℻ *876/993– 7133. 10 rooms. Restaurant, bar, in-room safes, no-smoking rooms, room service, pool, massage. AE, MC, V. CP, EP, MAP.*

$$ ⚅ **Jamaica Palace.** Built to resemble a 17th-century Italian mansion, this imposing and somewhat impersonal white-columned property has black-lacquer and gilded oversize furniture throughout its common areas. Some rooms are more lavish than others, though each has a semicircular bed, European objets d'art, Asian rugs; none are equipped with TVs (you can, however, rent one). Although the hotel isn't on the beach, there's a 114-ft swimming pool that's shaped like Jamaica. ⊠ *Williamsfield (Box 227),* ☎ *876/993–2021 or 800/423–4095 (reservations service),* ℻ *876/993–3459. 24 rooms, 56 suites. 3 restaurants, 2 bars, in-room safes, room service, pool, laundry service. AE, MC, V. CP, EP, MAP.*

$–$$ ⚅ **Dragon Bay.** Set on a private cove, Dragon Bay is an idyllic grouping of individually decorated villas surrounded by tropical gardens. Villa 35 has a private pool, a large living room, and two bedrooms with separate sitting rooms that have sofa beds. This place is popular with German and Italian tour groups. ⊠ *Dragon Bay (Box 176)*, ☎ *876/993– 8751 or 800/633–3284*, ℻ *876/993–3284. 30 1-, 2-, and 3-bedroom villas. 2 restaurants, 3 bars, refrigerators, room service, pool, massage, 2 tennis courts, aerobics, exercise room, volleyball, beach, dive shop, snorkeling. AE, MC, V. All-inclusive, EP, FAP, MAP.*

$ 🏨 **Bonnie View Plantation Hotel.** Accommodations here are spartan, mattresses are a tad lumpy, and the furnishings a bit frayed. But sublime views and tranquil air, rather than rooms and amenities, are the draws here. The nicest rooms (more expensive) are those with private verandas. But in any room you can open your window for a burst of invigorating mountain air. The restaurant also has unparalleled water panoramas. Beachcombers take note: It's a 25-minute drive to the ocean. ⊠ *Bonnie View Rd. (Box 82)*, ☎ *876/ 993–2752 or 800/423–4095*, ℻ *876/993–2862. 20 rooms. Restaurant, pool. AE, MC, V. EP.*

Runaway Bay

The smallest of the resort areas, Runaway Bay has a handful of modern hotels, a few new all-inclusive resorts, and an 18-hole golf course.

$$$$ 🏨 **FDR, Franklyn D. Resort.** Jamaica's first all-inclusive, family resort is the answer to parents' prayers. Upscale yet unpretentious, the complex has spacious, well-thought-out one, two-, and three-bedroom suites in pink villas set in a horseshoe around a pool. Best of all, a staff member is assigned to each suite, filling the role of nanny, housekeeper, and cook. Children and teens are kept busy with supervised activities and sports. Parents can join in the activities or just lounge by the pool, golf, or scuba dive. ⊠ *St. Ann's Bay (Box 201)*, ☎ *876/973–4591 or 800/654–1337 (reservations service)*, ℻ *876/973–3071. 76 suites. 2 restaurants, 3 bars, kitchenettes, pool, golf privileges, tennis court, beach, children's programs. AE, MC, V. All-inclusive.*

$$$$ 🏨 **Grand Lido Braco Village Resort.** Just a 15-minute drive
★ west of Runaway Bay, this all-inclusive, adults-only, gingerbread- and Georgian-style village (a member of the SuperClubs family) focuses on the culture, crafts, music, and food of Jamaica. Boutiques, an art shop, and several restau-

rants—including a jerk grill, a pastry shop, and a sidewalk café—fan out from a central fountain in the "town square." The meandering pool next to the white-sand beach is one of the largest in the country. Rooms, done in bright tropical colors, are generously sized, and all but a few (which have garden views) are steps from the 2,000-ft beach or have a great view of the ocean from a patio. ⊠ *Rio Bueno, Trelawny,* ☎ *876/954–0000 or 800/GO–SUPER (reservations service),* ℻ *876/954–0020. 232 rooms. 4 restaurants, 3 bars, café, in-room safes, pool, 2 hot tubs, 9-hole golf course, 2 tennis courts, hiking, soccer, beach, fishing, shops, dance club, theater. 3-night minimum stay. AE, DC, MC, V. All-inclusive, EP, FAP, MAP.*

$$$–
$$$$
★
🏨 **Breezes Golf and Beach Resort.** This moderately priced SuperClubs all-inclusive emphasizes an active, sports-oriented vacation—from golf (at the nearby 18-hole course), tennis, and horseback riding to an array of water sports. Expert instruction and top-rate equipment are part of the package. Rooms have white-tile floors, cozy love seats, TVs, carved wooden headboards, and big marble bathrooms. Guests—often Germans, Italians, and Japanese—flock here for the psychedelically colored reef just off the beach, as well as the superb golf school. ⊠ *North Coast Hwy. (Box 58),* ☎ *876/973–2436 or 800/859–7873 (reservations service),* ℻ *876/973–2352. 238 rooms, 4 suites. 2 restaurants, 4 bars, grill, in-room safes, 2 pools, 3 outdoor hot tubs, 2 tennis courts, golf privileges, horseback riding, beach. 3-night minimum stay. AE, DC, MC, V. All-inclusive.*

$$–$$$
🏨 **Club Caribbean.** Families, including many from Europe, are drawn to this all-inclusive complex of Caribbean cottages on a narrow beach. The rooms are simple and clean, with rattan furnishings and floral-print fabrics; some have kitchenettes. For more space, ask for a garden suite. Swings provide seating in the gazebo bar, a popular hangout around sunset. ⊠ *Box 65,* ☎ *876/973–3507 or 800/223–9815 (reservations service),* ℻ *876/973–3509. 135 rooms, 19 suites. Restaurant, 3 bars, in-room safes, pool, massage, 2 tennis courts, beach, children's programs, playground. AE, MC, V. All-inclusive.*

3 Dining

ALTHOUGH MANY CULTURES have contributed to Jamaica's cuisine, it has become a true cuisine in its own right—interesting, and ultimately rewarding. It would be a shame to travel to the heart of this complex culture without having at least one typical island meal.

Probably the most famous Jamaican dish is jerk pork—the ultimate island barbecue. The pork (purists cook a whole pig) is covered with a paste of Scotch bonnet peppers, pimento berries (also known as allspice), and other herbs and cooked slowly over a coal fire. Many aficionados believe that the best jerk comes from Boston Beach near Port Antonio. Jerked chicken and fish are also seen on many menus. The ever-so traditional rice and peas, also known as "coat of arms," is similar to the *moros y cristianos* of Spanish-speaking islands: white rice cooked with red kidney beans, coconut milk, scallions, and seasonings.

The island's most famous soup—the fiery pepper pot—is a peppery (of course) mixture of salt pork, salt beef, okra, and the island green known as callaloo. Patties (spicy meat pies) elevate street food to new heights. Although they actually originated in Haiti, Jamaicans excel at making them. Curry goat is another island standout: young goat is cooked with spices and is more tender and has a gentler flavor than the lamb for which it was substituted by immigrants from India. Salted fish was once the best islanders could eat between catches. Out of this necessity, the breakfast staple (and the national dish) of seasoned salt fish and ackee was invented. Ackee is a red fruit that grows on trees throughout the island, and when cooked, reminds most people of scrambled eggs.

Where restaurants are concerned, Kingston has the widest selection, with establishments that serve Italian, French, Cantonese, German, Thai, Indian, Korean, and Continental fare as well as Rasta natural foods. There are also fine restaurants in all the resort areas, many in the resorts themselves. Most restaurants outside the hotels in MoBay and Ocho Rios will provide complimentary transportation.

What to Wear

Dress is usually casual chic (or just casual at many local hangouts). There are a few exceptions in Kingston and at the top resorts, some of which require semiformal wear in the evening during high season. People tend to dress up for dinner—just because they feel like it—so men might be more comfortable in nice slacks, women in a sundress.

CATEGORY	COST*
$$$$	over $40
$$$	$30–$40
$$	$20–$30
$	Under $20

per person, excluding drinks, service, and tip

Kingston

ASIAN

$–$$ ✕ **Jade Garden.** On the third floor of the Sovereign Centre shopping mall, this establishment, with its shiny black-lacquer chairs and views of the Blue Mountains, garners rave reviews for its Cantonese and Thai menu. Favorites include steamed fish in black-bean sauce, black mushrooms stuffed with shrimp, and shrimp with lychee. Dim sum is served every Sunday afternoon. ⊠ *106 Hope Rd.,* ☎ *876/978–3476 or 876/978–3479. AE, MC, V.*

CONTINENTAL

$$$– ✕ **Blue Mountain Inn.** The elegant Blue Mountain Inn is a
$$$$ 30-minute taxi ride from New Kingston and worth every
★ penny of the fare. On a former coffee plantation, the antiques-laden inn complements its English colonial atmosphere with Continental cuisine. All the classic beef and seafood dishes are here, including chateaubriand béarnaise and lobster thermidor. ⊠ *Gordon Town Rd.,* ☎ *876/927–1700 or 876/927–2606. Reservations essential. Jacket required. AE, MC, V. Closed Sun. No lunch.*

$$$– ✕ **Palm Court.** Nestled on the mezzanine floor of the Wynd-
$$$$ ham New Kingston (☞ Chapter 2), the elegant Palm Court is open for lunch and dinner. The menu is Continental; the rack of lamb, sautéed snapper almandine, and grilled salmon are very tasty. ⊠ *75 Knutsford Blvd.,* ☎ *876/926–5430. AE, DC, MC, V. No lunch weekends.*

38

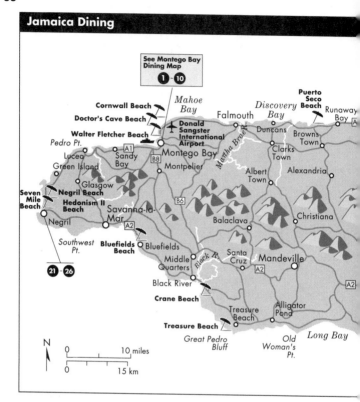

Jamaica Dining

See Montego Bay
Dining Map
1 - **10**

*Mahoe
Bay*

Cornwall Beach
Doctor's Cave Beach
Walter Fletcher Beach
Pedro Pt.

**Donald
Sangster
International
Airport**
Falmouth

*Puerto
Seco* Beach Runaway
Discovery Bay
Bay

Lucea
Green Island
Sandy
Bay
Montego Bay
Montpelier
Duncans
Browns
Town
Clarks
Town
Albert
Town
Alexandria

Glasgow
A1
B8

**Seven
Mile
Beach**
Negril Beach
**Hedonism II
Beach**
Savanna-la-
Mar
Negril
B6
Balaclava
Christiana

*Southwest
Pt.*
**Bluefields
Beach**
A2
Bluefields
Middle
Quarters
Santa
Cruz
Mandeville
A2

21 - **26**
Black River
A2

Crane Beach

Treasure Beach
Treasure
Beach
Alligator
Pond

*Great Pedro
Bluff*
*Old
Woman's
Pt.*
Long Bay

N
0   10 miles
0   15 km

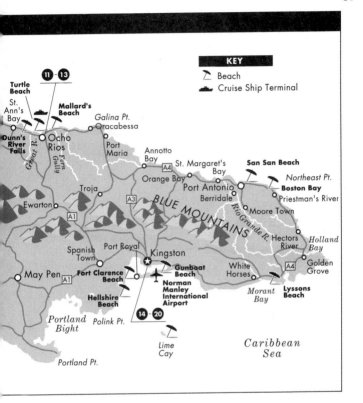

KEY
- Beach
- Cruise Ship Terminal

⓫ - ⓭

Turtle Beach

St. Ann's Bay

Mallard's Beach

Galina Pt.

Dunn's River Falls

Oracabessa

Ocho Rios

Great R.

Fern Gully

Port Maria

Annotto Bay

St. Margaret's Bay

San San Beach

Northeast Pt.

Orange Bay

Port Antonio

Boston Bay

Troja

Berridale

Priestman's River

A4

A3

BLUE MOUNTAINS

Moore Town

Rio Grande R.

Ewarton

A1

Hectors River

Holland Bay

Spanish Town

Port Royal

Kingston

Golden Grove

Fort Clarence Beach

Gunboat Beach

White Horses

A4

May Pen

A1

Norman Manley International Airport

Hellshire Beach

Morant Bay

Lyssons Beach

⓮ - ⓴

Portland Bight

Polink Pt.

Lime Cay

Caribbean Sea

Portland Pt.

ECLECTIC

$$$– ╳ **Ivor Guest House.** This elegant yet cozy restaurant is in
$$$$ an 1870s home in the hills 2,000 ft above sea level. Go for
dinner, when the view is dramatically caught between shim-
mering stars and the glittering lights of Kingston. Interna-
tional cuisine with Jamaican flare is served in prix-fixe
four-course dinners that average $35 per person. Owner
Helen Aitken is an animated and cordial hostess. Afternoon
tea here is a treat. There are three antiques-furnished guest
rooms for those who want more time in this tranquil spot.
⊠ *Jack's Hill,* ☎ *876/702–0510 or 876/702–0276. Reser-
vations essential. AE, MC, V.*

JAMAICAN

$–$$ ╳ **Peppers.** This casual outdoor bar with picnic tables is
the *in* spot in Kingston. It's slow during weekday afternoons
but frenetic on Friday night and Saturday. Sample the
grilled lobster or jerk pork and chicken with the local Red
Stripe beer, sit back and enjoy the local reggae band. ⊠ *31
Upper Waterloo Rd.,* ☎ *876/925–2219. MC, V. Closed Sun.*

$ ╳ **Hot Pot.** Jamaicans love the Hot Pot for breakfast, lunch,
★ and dinner. Fricassee chicken is the specialty, along with other
local dishes, such as mackerel run-down (salted mackerel
cooked with coconut milk and spices) and ackee and salted
cod. The restaurant's fresh juices "in season" are the best—
tamarind, sorrel, coconut water, soursop, and cucumber.
⊠ *2 Altamont Terr.,* ☎ *876/929–3906. MC, V.*

Montego Bay

ECLECTIC

$$–$$$ ╳ **Day-O Plantation Restaurant.** Transport yourself back
in time with a fine meal served on the garden terrace of this
Georgian-style plantation house. Start with smoked marlin, then segue into seafood ragout, broiled rock lobster with
lemon butter, or beef fillet with béarnaise sauce. Sweeten
things up with one of the traditional Jamaican desserts
(rum pudding, sweet cakes, or fruit salad). ⊠ *Beside Barnett Estate Plantation, Fairfield,* ☎ *876/952–1825. AE, MC,
V. Closed Mon.*

$$–$$$ ╳ **Sugar Mill.** Seafood is served with flair at this terrace
★ restaurant on the golf course of the Half Moon Golf, Ten-

nis, and Beach Club (☞ Chapter 2). Caribbean specialties, steak, and lobster are usually offered in a pungent sauce that blends Dijon mustard with Jamaica's own Pickapeppa sauce. Otherwise, choices are the daily à la carte specials and anything flamed. Live music and a well-stocked wine cellar round out the experience. ☒ *7 mi east of MoBay,* ☎ *876/953–2228. Dinner reservations essential. AE, MC, V.*

$–$$ ✕ **Margueritaville Caribbean Bar and Grill.** This brightly painted bar-restaurant is tough to miss: just look for the slide that connects it with the water. You'll find plenty of casual dishes on the menu, including burgers, chicken sandwiches, tuna melts, pizza, and the like. ☒ *Gloucester Ave.,* ☎ *876/952–4777. AE, MC, V.*

$–$$ ✕ **The Native.** This open-air stone terrace, shaded by a large poinciana tree and overlooking Gloucester Avenue, serves Jamaican and international dishes. To go native, start with smoked marlin, move on to the *boonoonoonoos* platter (a sampler of local dishes), and round out with coconut pie or *duckanoo* (a sweet dumpling of cornmeal, coconut, and banana wrapped in a banana leaf and steamed). Caesar salad, seafood linguine, and shrimp kabobs are fine alternatives. Live entertainment and candlelit tables make this a romantic choice for dinner on weekends. The popular afternoon buffets on Friday and Sunday are family affairs. ☒ *29 Gloucester Ave.,* ☎ *876/979–2769. Dinner reservations essential. AE, MC, V.*

$–$$ ✕ **Town House.** Most of the rich and famous who have visited Jamaica over the decades have eaten here. You'll find daily specials, delicious variations of standard dishes (red snapper *papillote* is a specialty, with lobster, cheese, and wine sauce), and many Jamaican favorites (curried chicken with breadfruit and ackee). The 18th-century Georgian house is adorned with original Jamaican and Haitian art. There's alfresco dining on the stone patio. ☒ *16 Church St.,* ☎ *876/952–2660. Dinner reservations essential. AE, DC, MC, V. No lunch Sun.*

$ ✕ **Le Chalet.** Don't let the French name fool you. This
★ Denny's look-alike, set in a nondescript shopping mall, serves heaping helpings of some of the best Chinese and Jamaican food in MoBay. Tasty lobster Cantonese costs only $15. ☒ *32 Gloucester Ave.,* ☎ *876/952–5240. AE, MC, V. No lunch Sun.*

Montego Bay Dining

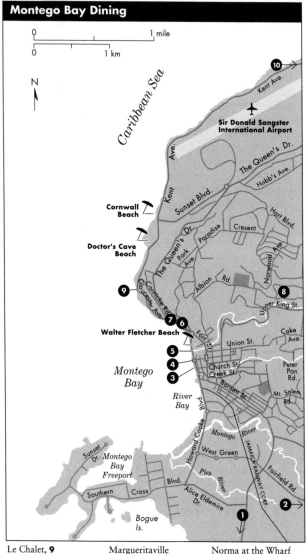

Le Chalet, **9**
Day-O Plantation Restaurant, **2**
Julia's Italian Restaurant, **7**

Margueritaville Caribbean Bar and Grill, **6**
Marguerites, **7**
The Native, **5**

Norma at the Wharf House, **1**
Pier 1, **3**
Sugar Mill, **10**
Town House, **4**

ITALIAN

$$$– X Julia's Italian Restaurant. Couples flock to this romantic
$$$$ Italian restaurant in the hills overlooking MoBay. You can
choose from an à la carte menu or order a five-course prix-
fixe meal ($33–$45 per person) that includes homemade soups
and pastas; entrées of fish, chicken, and veal; and scrump-
tious desserts. Don't expect the meal to equal the stupendous
view, and you won't be disappointed. ⊠ *Bogue Hill,* ☎
876/952–1772. Reservations essential. AE, MC, V.

JAMAICAN

$$–$$$ X Norma at the Wharf House. This sister property to cre-
ative chef-entrepreneur Norma's successful Kingston restau-
rant has gathered rave reviews as a supper club. The setting
is a converted 300-year-old, stone, sugar warehouse on
the water, decorated in blue and white. Innovative Ja-
maican cuisine ranges from Caribbean lobster steamed in
Red Stripe beer to jerk chicken with mangoes flambé. ⊠
10 minutes west of MoBay in Reading, ☎ *876/979–2745.
Dinner reservations essential. MC, V. Closed Mon. and
May–Aug.*

SEAFOOD

$$$ X Marguerites. This romantic pierside dining room spe-
cializes in seafood. Flambé is the operative word here: lob-
ster, shrimp, fish, and several desserts are prepared in
dancing flames as you sip on an exotic cocktail. The Cae-
sar salad, prepared tableside, is also a treat. ⊠ *Gloucester
Ave.,* ☎ *876/952–4777. Reservations essential. AE, MC,
V. No lunch.*

$$–$$$ X Pier 1. After tropical drinks at the deck bar, you'll be
ready to dig into the international variations on fresh
seafood, the best of which are the grilled lobster and any
preparation of island snapper. Several party cruises leave
from the marina here, and on Friday night the restaurant
is mobbed by locals who come to dance. ⊠ *Just off Howard
Cooke Blvd.,* ☎ *876/952–2452. AE, MC, V.*

Negril

CARIBBEAN/CREOLE

$ X Sweet Spice. This mom-and-pop diner run by the Whytes
serves inexpensive, generous plates of conch, fried or cur-

ried chicken, freshly caught fish, oxtail in brown stew sauce, and other down-home specialties. The fresh juices are quite satisfying. Drop by for breakfast, lunch, or dinner. ⊠ *1 White Hall Rd.,* ☎ *876/957–4621. Reservations not accepted. MC, V.*

ECLECTIC

$$ ✕ **Marguerritaville.** Set on a beautiful stretch of Seven Mile
★   Beach, this operation, a sibling of the wildly popular Marguerritaville in MoBay, is a sports bar, a disco, a beach club, and a restaurant. There is also an art gallery, a gift shop, a five-star PADI dive shop, volleyball and basketball courts, and changing rooms so that you can slip out of your wet suit. Lobster is the house specialty. Far less expensive are the fish, chicken, and sandwich platters. There are also more than 50 margaritas from which to choose. ⊠ *Norman Manley Blvd.,* ☎ *876/957–4467. AE, MC, V.*

$$ ✕ **Tan-ya's.** This alfresco restaurant overlooks the pool and hot tub at Sea Splash Resort, an intimate, 15-suite property surrounded by palm trees on lovely Seven Mile Beach. Jamaican delicacies with an international flavor are served for breakfast, lunch, and dinner. Try the excellent deviled crab backs or the smoked marlin. ⊠ *Norman Manley Blvd.,* ☎ *876/957–4041. AE, DC, MC, V.*

$–$$ ✕ **Rick's Cafe.** Here it is, the local landmark complete with cliffs, cliff divers, and powerful sunsets, all perfectly choreographed. Most folks come for the drinks and the renowned sunset party, since the standard pub menu is overpriced. In the sunset ritual, the crowd toasts Mother Nature with rum drinks amid shouts, laughter, and ever-shifting meeting and greeting. When the sun slips below the horizon, there are more shouts, more cheers, and more rounds of rum. ⊠ *West End Rd.,* ☎ *876/957–0380. MC, V.*

$ ✕ **Kuyaba on the Beach.** This charming thatch-roof eatery features an international menu—including curried conch, kingfish steak, grilled lamb with sautéed mushrooms, and an array of pasta dishes—and a lively ambience, especially at the bar. There's a crafts shop on the premises, and chaise lounges line the beach; come prepared to spend some time, and don't forget a towel and bathing suit. ⊠ *Norman Manley Blvd.,* ☎ *876/957–4318. AE, MC, V.*

SEAFOOD

$–$$ ✕ **Cosmo's Seafood Restaurant and Bar.** Owner Cosmo
★ Brown has made this seaside open-air bistro a pleasant place
to spend the afternoon—and maybe stay on for dinner. Fish
is the main attraction, and the conch soup—a house specialty—is a meal in itself. You'll also find lobster (grilled
or curried), fish-and-chips, and a catch-of-the-morning.
Customers often drop cover-ups to take a dip before coffee and dessert and return to lounge in chairs scattered under
almond and seagrape trees. (There's a small entrance fee
for the beach.) ⊠ *Norman Manley Blvd.,* ☎ 876/957–4330.
Reservations not accepted. AE, MC, V.

Ocho Rios

ECLECTIC

$$$– ✕ **Almond Tree.** One of the most popular restaurants in
$$$$ Ocho Rios, the Almond Tree has a menu of Jamaican and
★ Continental favorites: pumpkin and pepper-pot soups, and
many wonderful preparations of fresh fish, veal piccata, and
fondue. The swinging rope chairs of the terrace bar and the
tables perched above a lovely Caribbean cove are great fun.
⊠ *83 Main St.,* ☎ 876/974–2813. *Dinner reservations es-
sential. AE, DC, MC, V.*

$–$$ ✕ **Evita's.** The setting here is a hilltop 1860s gingerbread
★ house. Large, open windows open to cooling mountain
breezes and stunning views of city and sea. More than 30
kinds of pasta are served, ranging from lasagna Rastafari
(vegetarian) and fiery "jerk" spaghetti to *rotelle colombo*
(crabmeat with white sauce and noodles). There are also
excellent fish dishes—sautéed fillet of red snapper with orange sauce, scampi and lobster in basil cream sauce, red
snapper stuffed with crabmeat—and several meat dishes,
among them a tasty grilled sirloin with mushroom sauce.
Kids under 12 eat for half price, and light eaters will appreciate half-portion orders. ⊠ *Mantalent Inn, Eden Bower
Rd.,* ☎ 876/974–2333. *AE, MC, V.*

$–$$ ✕ **Little Pub.** Alfresco dining in a village-square setting
awaits you at this charming restaurant. It also has a bustling
sports bar and an energetic Caribbean review several nights
a week. Jamaican standards (jerk or curried chicken, baked
crab, sautéed snapper) accompany surf and turf, lobster ther-

midor, pasta primavera, seafood stir-fry, crêpe suzette, and bananas flambé. Burgers and other standard pub fare are also available. ⊠ *59 Main St.,* ☎ *876/974–2324. AE, MC, V.*

JAMAICAN

$ ✕ **Ocho Rios Village Jerk Centre.** This blue-canopied, open-
★ air eatery is a good place to park yourself for frosty Red Stripe beer and fiery jerk pork, chicken, or seafood. Milder barbecued meats, also sold by weight (typically ¼ or ½ pound make good servings), also turn up on the fresh daily chalkboard menu posted on the wall. It's lively at lunch, especially when passengers from cruise ships swamp the place. ⊠ *DaCosta Dr.,* ☎ *876/974–2549. MC, V.*

4 Beaches, Outdoor Activities, and Sports

BEACHES

Jamaica has 200 mi of beaches, some of them relatively deserted. Generally, the farther west you go, the lighter and finer the sand. The beaches listed below are public (though there's usually a small admission charge) and are among Jamaica's best. Nearly every resort has its own private beach, complete with towels and water sports. Some of the larger resorts sell day passes to nonguests.

Discovery Bay

Puerto Seco Beach is a stretch of sand that's frequented primarily by locals. There's an admission charge of $5 for the beach, which is open daily 9–5. You'll find plenty of watersports activities and some concessions that sell local foods.

Kingston Area

As a rule, the beaches outside Kingston are not as beautiful as those in the resort areas. **Fort Clarence,** in the Hellshire Hills area southwest of the city, has changing facilities and entertainment. **Hellshire Beach,** in Bridgeport, about a 20- to 30-minute drive from Kingston, is very popular. You'll find food vendors, changing rooms, and plenty of (recorded) music. You can reach **Lime Cay** by boat (which you can hire at Morgan's Harbor Marina in Port Royal for a small fee). This island, just beyond Kingston Harbor, is perfect for picnicking, sunning, and swimming. **Lyssons Beach,** in Morant Bay, sometimes lures Kingstonians 32 mi east of the city to its lovely golden sand.

Montego Bay

Cornwall Beach is a lively beach with lots of places that sell food and drink as well as a water-sports concession. The 5-mi **Doctor's Cave Beach** has been spotlighted in so many travel articles and brochures that it often resembles Fort Lauderdale during spring break. On the bright side, it has much to offer admirers beyond just sugary sand, including changing rooms, colorful if overly insistent vendors, and plenty of places to grab a snack. **Rose Hall Beach Club,** east of central MoBay near Rose Hall Great House, is a secluded area with changing rooms and showers, a water-sports center, volleyball and other beach games, and a beach bar and grill. **Walter Fletcher Beach,** near the center of town, offers protection from the surf on a windy day and, therefore, unusually fine swimming; the calm waters make it a good bet for children.

Negril

Not too long ago **Seven Mile Beach** was a beachcomber's Eden. Today much of its white sand is fronted by resorts, although some stretches along Bloody Bay remain relatively untouched. In sections where there are no hotels, there are some nude beach areas, such as one adjacent to Cosmo's (☞ Chapter 3). A few resorts have built accommodations overlooking their nude beaches, thereby adding a new dimension to the traditional notion of "ocean view."

Ocho Rios

Turtle Beach, stretching behind Renaissance Jamaica Grande and Club Jamaica, is the busiest beach in Ocho Rios (where the islanders go to swim). **James Bond Beach,** east of Ocho Rios in the quaint village of Oracabessa, was opened in 1997 and has become a favorite, owing to the live reggae performances on the bandstand here.

Port Antonio

Boston Bay, approximately 11 mi east of Port Antonio, beyond the Blue Lagoon, is a small, intimate beach. It's a good place to buy the famous peppery delicacy, jerk pork, available at any of the shacks spewing scented smoke along the beach. **San San Beach,** about 5 mi east of Port Antonio, has beautiful blue waters and is used mainly by area villa or hotel owners and their guests.

The South Coast

To find a beach off the main tourist routes, head for Jamaica's unexploited south coast. **Bluefields Beach,** near Savanna-La-Mar (or just Sav-La-Mar to locals), south of Negril, is nearest to "civilization." **Crane Beach,** at Black River, has retained its natural beauty and has—so far—remained undiscovered by most tourists. **Treasure Beach** has to be the best that the south shore has to offer. Set by a quaint fishing village, this undeveloped beach has coves that are ideal for snorkeling explorations. These isolated beaches are some of the island's safest because the population is sparse in this region and hasslers are practically nonexistent. You should, however, use common-sense precautions; never leave valuables unattended on the beach.

OUTDOOR ACTIVITIES AND SPORTS

The tourist board licenses all recreational activity operators and outfitters, which should ensure you of fair business practices as long as you deal with companies that display the decals.

Bird-Watching

Many bird-watchers flock here for the chance to see the vervain hummingbird (the second smallest bird in the world, larger only than Cuba's bee hummingbird), the Jamaican tody (which nests underground), or another of the island's 27 endemic species. A great place to spot birds is the **Rocklands Feeding Station** (⊠ Anchovy, south of Montego Bay, ☎ 876/952–2009). In Mandeville, tours of the bird sanctuary at **Marshall's Penn Great House** (☎ 876/963–8569) are by appointment only and are led by owner Robert Sutton, one of Jamaica's leading ornithologists.

Fishing

Port Antonio makes deep-sea fishing headlines with its annual Blue Marlin Tournament, and Montego Bay and Ocho Rios have devotees who exchange tales (tall and otherwise) about sailfish, yellowfin tuna, wahoo, dolphinfish, and bonito. Licenses aren't required, and you can arrange to charter a boat at your hotel. A boat (with captain, crew, and equipment) that accommodates four to six passengers costs about $400 for a half day.

Golf

Golfers appreciate both the beauty and the challenges offered by Jamaica's courses. Caddies are mandatory throughout the island, and rates are $5–$15. Cart rentals are available at all courses except Constant Spring and the Manchester Club; costs are $20–$35.

Good Kingston courses include **Caymanas** (⊠ 6 mi west of Kingston, ☏ 876/997–8026), Jamaica's first major championship 18-hole course (greens fee is $53), and **Constant Spring** (⊠ A3, Constant Spring, ☏ 876/924–1610), a short 18-hole course designed in 1920 (greens fee is $53).

MANDEVILLE

A 9-hole course in the hills, the **Manchester Club** (⊠ Caledonia Rd. and Ward Ave., ☏ 876/962–2403) is the Caribbean's oldest golf course, and has a greens fee of $14.

MONTEGO BAY

Some of the best courses are in Montego Bay. **Tryall Golf, Tennis, and Beach Club** (⊠ 15 mi west of MoBay on North Coast Hwy., ☏ 876/956–5681) has an 18-hole championship course on the site of a 19th-century sugar plantation (greens fees run $40–$60 for guests, $100–$125 for nonguests). **Half Moon Golf, Tennis, and Beach Club**'s (⊠ 7 mi east of MoBay, ☏ 876/953–3105) 18-hole course is the home of the Red Stripe Pro Am and was designed by Robert Trent Jones (the greens fee is $95). **Wyndham Rose Hall** (⊠ 4 mi east of airport on North Coast Hwy., ☏ 876/953–2650) hosts invitational tournaments (fees run $50–$60). **Ironshore** (⊠ 3 mi east of airport, ☏ 876/953–2800) has an 18-hole links-style course (the greens fee is $45).

NEGRIL

The **Anancy Family Fun and Nature Park** (⊠ Norman Manley Blvd., ☏ 876/957–5100) has an 18-hole minigolf course. **Grand Lido Braco Village Resort** (⊠ Trelawny, between Duncans and Rio Bueno, ☏ 876/954–0000) is a 9-hole course with lush vegetation (nonguests should call for fee information). Great golf, rolling hills, and a "liquor mobile" go hand in hand at the 18-hole **Negril Hills Golf Club** (⊠ East of Negril on Sheffield Rd., ☏ 876/957–4638); the greens fee is $58.

OCHO RIOS

Prospect Plantation (⊠ A3, 3 mi east of Ocho Rios, ☏ 876/994–1058) has an 18-hole minigolf course. **Sandals Golf and Country Club** (⊠ 2 mi east of Ocho Rios, ☏ 876/975–

0119) has an 18-hole course 700 ft above sea level (the greens fee is $70 for nonguests).

Breezes Golf Club (⊠ North Coast Hwy., ☎ 876/973–2561) has an 18-hole course that has hosted many championship events (greens fees are $58 for nonguests).

Horseback Riding

Jamaica is fortunate to have an outstanding equestrian facility: **Chukka Cove** (☎ 876/972–2506) near Ocho Rios. This resort offers instruction in riding, polo, and jumping, as well as hour-long trail rides, three-hour beach rides, and six-hour rides to a restored great house. During in-season weekends this is the place for polo (and social) action. You can also saddle up at the **Rocky Point Riding Stables at Half Moon** (☎ 876/953–2286), which is just east of the Half Moon Club in Montego Bay; the **Barnett Estate Great House** (☎ 876/952–2382) in Montego Bay; and the **Prospect Plantation** (☎ 876/994–1058) in Ocho Rios.

Scuba Diving and Snorkeling

The major areas for scuba diving and snorkeling are Negril in the west and Port Antonio in the east. MoBay is also known for its wall dives. All the large resorts rent equipment, and the all-inclusive places have scuba diving on their lists of activities included in the rate.

Although **scuba** (the word is derived from what was once an acronym for "self-contained underwater breathing apparatus") diving is surprisingly simple, *call your physician before your vacation, and make sure that you have no condition that should prevent you from diving!* A full checkup is an excellent idea, especially if you're over 30. Since it is dangerous to travel on a plane after diving, schedule your diving courses and travel plans accordingly.

Learning to dive with a reputable instructor is a must. In addition to teaching you how to resurface properly, a qualified instructor can train you to read "dive tables," the charts that calculate how long you can safely stay at certain depths. Many resorts offer courses consisting of two to three hours of instruction on land and time in a swimming pool or waist-deep water to get used to the mouthpiece and hose (the regulator) and the mask. A shallow (20-ft), supervised dive from a boat or beach follows.

You can earn a certification card—often called a C-card—from an accredited diving organization: NAUI, CMAS, NASE, or PADI. PADI (Professional Association of Diving Instructors) offers a free list of training facilities (☞ Diving *in* Essential Information).

Snorkeling requires no special skills, and many establishments that rent equipment will teach you the basics. As with any water sport, it's never a good idea to snorkel alone. You don't have to be a great swimmer to snorkel, but occasionally currents come up that require stamina. Time seems to slow down underwater, so wear a water-resistant watch and let someone on land know when to expect you back. Remember that taking souvenirs—shells, pieces of coral, interesting rocks—is forbidden. Many reefs are legally protected marine parks, where removal of living shells is prohibited because it upsets the ecology.

The following operators offer certification courses and dive trips as well as snorkel gear rentals and are licensed by the tourist board:

MONTEGO BAY

North Coast Marine Sports (⊠ Several locations in Montego Bay, ☎ 876/953–2211). **Resort Divers** (⊠ Gloucester Ave., Montego Bay, ☎ 876/952–4285).

NEGRIL

Dolphin Divers (⊠ Norman Manley Blvd., Negril, ☎ 876/957–4944). **Negril Scuba Centre** (⊠ Negril Beach Club, Norman Manley Blvd., Negril, ☎ 876/957–4425). **Sandals Beach Resort Watersports** (⊠ Norman Manley Blvd., Negril, ☎ 876/957–5216).

OCHO RIOS

Garfield Diving Station (⊠ Shop 13, Santa Maria, west of Renaissance Jamaica Grande, Ocho Rios, ☎ 876/974–

5749). **Resort Divers** (⊠ 1 Carib Arcade, Ocho Rios, ☎ 876/974–5338).

PORT ANTONIO

Lady G'Diver (⊠ San San Beach, Port Antonio, ☎ 876/993–3281) also offers windsurfing, glass-bottom boating, and sailing (excursions start at $25 per person).

RUNAWAY BAY

Resort Divers (⊠ Breezes Golf and Beach Resort, North Coast Hwy., Runaway Bay, ☎ 876/973–5750).

Tennis

Many hotels have tennis facilities that are free to their guests, and some will allow nonguests to play for a fee.

KINGSTON

The **Crowne Plaza** (☎ 876/925–7676), the **Le Méridien Pegasus** (☎ 876/926–3690), and the **Wyndham New Kingston** (☎ 876/926–5430) all have courts for guest use.

MONTEGO BAY

The sport is a highlight at **Tryall Golf, Tennis, and Beach Club** (⊠ 15 mi west of MoBay on North Coast Hwy., ☎ 876/956–5660). **Round Hill Hotel and Villas** (⊠ 8 mi west of MoBay on North Coast Hwy., ☎ 876/952–5150) has five courts. **Sandals Montego Bay** (⊠ Kent Ave., ☎ 876/952–5510) has four courts lit for night play and a tennis pro. **Half Moon Golf, Tennis, and Beach Club** (⊠ 7 mi east of MoBay, ☎ 876/953–2211) has 13 Laykold tennis courts (seven lit for night play) along with a pro and a pro shop.

NEGRIL

You'll find five hard courts and five clay courts, all lit for night play, at **Swept Away** (⊠ Norman Manley Blvd., ☎ 876/957–4040).

OCHO RIOS

Sandals Dunn's River (⊠ North Coast Hwy., ☎ 876/972–1610), has four courts lit for night play as well as the services of a pro. **Grand Lido Sans Souci** also has four lighted courts and a pro (⊠ North Coast Hwy., 2 mi east of Ocho

Rios, ☎ 876/974–2353). At **Ciboney, Ocho Rios** (✉ 104 Main St., Ocho Rios, ☎ 876/974–1027) you'll find a pro and six lighted courts (three clay and three hard).

RUNAWAY BAY

Breezes Golf and Beach Resort (✉ North Coast Hwy., ☎ 876/973–2436) has two courts.

5 Shopping

SHOPPING HERE goes two ways: things Jamaican and things imported. Jamaican crafts are made with style and skill and take the form of resort wear, hand-loomed fabrics, silk screens, wood carvings, paintings, and other fine arts. Jamaican rum is a great take-home gift. So is Tia Maria, Jamaica's world-famous coffee liqueur. The same goes for the island's prized Blue Mountain and High Mountain coffees and its jams, jellies, and marmalades. If you shop around, you'll find good deals on such duty-free luxury items as jewelry, cameras, china, Swiss watches, and Irish crystal. The top-selling French perfumes are sold alongside Jamaica's own fragrances.

Shopping Areas and Malls

A shopping tour of the **Kingston** area should begin at Constant Spring Road or King Street. No matter where you start, keep in mind that shopping malls have caught on here with a fever. The ever-growing roster includes Twin Gates Plaza, New Lane Plaza, the New Kingston Shopping Centre, Tropical Plaza, Manor Park Plaza, the Village, the Springs, and the newest (and some say nicest), Sovereign Shopping Centre. Devon House is the place to find old and new Jamaica. The great house is now a museum with antiques and furniture reproductions; boutiques and an ice cream shop—try one of the tropical flavors (mango, guava, pineapple, and passion fruit)—now fill what were once the stables.

In **MoBay,** you should visit the "crafts market" on Market Street; just be prepared for haggling over prices in the midst of pandemonium. If you want to spend serious money, head for City Centre Plaza; Half Moon Village; Holiday Inn Shopping Centre; St. James's Place; Westgate Plaza; and Montego Bay Shopping Center, a favorite with locals.

Unless there's a cruise ship in port, the crafts markets in **Ocho Rios** are less hectic than the one in MoBay. The area's shopping plazas are Pineapple Place, Ocean Village, the Taj Mahal, Coconut Grove, and Island Plaza. The crafts markets in **Port Antonio** and **Negril** are good fun: you'll find a plethora of T-shirts; straw hats, baskets, and place mats; carved wood statues; colorful Rasta berets; and cheap jewelry.

Specialty Items

Clothes

Vaz Enterprises, LTD. (⊠ 77 East St., Kingston, ☎ 876/922–9200), the manufacturing outlet of designer Sonia Vaz, sells teeny-weeny bikinis. They're also for sale at several resorts.

Coffee

In Kingston, you'll find Blue Mountain coffee at **John R. Wong's Supermarket** (⊠ 1–5 Tobago Ave., ☎ 876/926–4811). **Magic Kitchen Ltd.** (⊠ Village Plaza, ☎ 876/926–8894) sells the magic beans. The **Sovereign Supermarket** (⊠ Sovereign Center, 106 Hope Rd., ☎ 876/978–1254) has a wide selection of coffee and other goods. In Negril, java lovers will find beans and ground coffee at **Hi-Lo Supermarket** (⊠ West End Rd., ☎ 876/957–4546). If the stores are out of Blue Mountain, you may have to settle for High Mountain coffee, the locals' second-preferred brand.

Handicrafts

Caribatik (⊠ A–1, 2 mi east of Falmouth, ☎ 876/954–3314), the studio of the late Muriel Chandler, stocks silk batiks, by the yard or made into chic designs. Drawing on patterns in nature, Chandler translated the birds, seascapes, flora, and fauna into works of art.

Gallery of West Indian Art (⊠ 1 Orange La., Montego Bay, ☎ 876/956–7050, ext. 312; ⊠ Round Hill, ☎ 876/952–5150) is the place to find Jamaican and Haitian paintings. A corner of the gallery is devoted to hand-turned pottery (some painted) and beautifully carved and painted birds and animals.

Harmony Hall (⊠ 8-minute drive east on A–1 from Ocho Rios, ☎ 876/975–4222), a restored great house, is where Annabella Proudlock sells her unique wooden boxes (their covers are decorated with reproductions of Jamaican paintings). Also on sale—and magnificently displayed—are larger reproductions of paintings, lithographs, and signed prints of Jamaican scenes and hand-carved, wooden combs. In addition, Harmony Hall is well-known for its art shows by local artists.

Ital-Craft (⌧ Upper Manor Park Shopping Plaza, 184C Spring Rd., Kingston, ☎ 876/931–0477) sells belts, bangles, and beads. Although Ital-Craft's handmade treasures are sold in boutiques throughout Jamaica, this, the factory location, has an outstanding selection of the belts, which are made of spectacular shells as well as leather, feathers, or fur. (The most ornate creations sell for about $75.) You'll also find some intriguing jewelry and purses here.

Magic Toys (☎ 875/990–6030) has a large studio in Mandeville, though the company's creations are seen in the resorts throughout the Caribbean. Gift items include jigsaw puzzles, mirrors, picture frames, and magnets—each item featuring a tropical design such as a parrot fish, a bird of paradise, or Jamaica's own doctor bird.

Things Jamaican (⌧ Devon House, 26 Hope Rd., Kingston, ☎ 876/929–6602; ⌧ 44 Fort St., Montego Bay, ☎ 876/952–5605) sells some of the best Jamaican crafts—from carved wooden bowls and trays to reproductions of silver and brass period pieces.

Jewelry

L. A. Henriques (⌧ Shop 12, Upper Manor Park Plaza, Kingston, ☎ 876/931–0613) sells high-quality jewelry made to order.

Liquor and Tobacco

As a rule, only rum distilleries, such as Sangster's, have better deals than the airport stores. Best of all, if you buy your rum or Tia Maria at either the Kingston or the MoBay airport before you leave, you don't have to tote all those heavy, breakable bottles to your hotel and then home again. Fine handmade Macanudo cigars make great easy-to-pack gifts; why not pick some up at Montego Bay airport on your way home? If you get the urge to puff during your stay, call 876/925–1082 for outlet information.

Records

In Negril, music buffs should check out **Countryside** (⌧ Hi-Lo Shopping Centre, Negril, ☎ 876/957–4538). If you like reggae by world-famous Jamaican artists—Bob Marley, Ziggy Marley, Peter Tosh, and Third World, to name a few—

a pilgrimage to **Randy's Record Mart** (⊠ 17 N. Parade, Kingston, ☎ 876/922–4859) is a must.

Also worth checking out are **De Muzic Shop** (⊠ Island Plaza, Ocho Rios, ☎ 876/974–9500), **Record City** (⊠ 1 William St., Port Antonio, ☎ 876/993–2836), **Record Plaza** (⊠ Tropical Plaza, Kingston, ☎ 876/926–7645), and **Top Ranking Records** (⊠ Westgate Plaza, Montego Bay, ☎ 876/952–1216).

Shoes

Cheap sandals are good buys in shopping centers throughout Jamaica. Although workmanship and leathers don't rival the craftsmanship of those found in Italy or Spain, neither do the prices (about $20 a pair). In Kingston, **Jacaranda** (⊠ Devon House, ☎ 876/929–6602) is a good place to sandal shop as is **Lee's Fifth Avenue Shoes** (⊠ Tropical Plaza, ☎ 876/926–7486). In Ocho Rios, the **Pretty Feet Shoe Shop** (⊠ Ocean Village Shopping Centre, ☎ 876/974–5040) is a good bet. In Montego Bay, try **Westgate Plaza.**

6 Nightlife

JAMAICA—ESPECIALLY KINGSTON—supports a lively community of musicians. For starters there's reggae, popularized by the late Bob Marley and the Wailers and performed today by son Ziggy Marley, Jimmy Tosh (the late Peter Tosh's son), Gregory Isaacs, Third World, Jimmy Cliff, and many others. If your experience of Caribbean music has been limited to steel drums and Harry Belafonte, then the political, racial, and religious messages of reggae may set you on your ear; listen closely and you just might hear the heartbeat of the people.

Those who know and love reggae should visit in mid-July to August for the Reggae Sunsplash. This four-night concert—at the Bob Marley Performing Center (a field set up with a temporary stage) in the Freeport area of Montego Bay—showcases local talent and attracts such big-name performers as Rick James, Gladys Knight and the Pips, Steel Pulse, Third World, and Ziggy Marley and the Melody Makers.

Evening entertainment also includes theatrical and dance shows. Although many resorts offer a "native night" with dances and limbo shows, for true Jamaican culture you should see a stage show in Kingston. Recommended are performances by the National Chorale of Jamaica, the Jamaica Folk Singers, and the National Dance Theater Company. For schedules, check with the tourist board (☞ Visitor Information *in* Essential Information).

Dance and Music Clubs

For the most part, the liveliest late-night happenings throughout Jamaica are in the major resort hotels. Some of the all-inclusives offer a dinner and disco pass from about $50. Pick up a copy of *The Daily Gleaner, The Jamaica Observer,* or *The Star* (available at newsstands throughout the island) for listings on who's playing and when and where. For venues with live reggae bands, expect to pay a $3–$10 cover charge.

BONUS MILES MAKE GREAT SOUVENIRS.

Earn Miles With Your MCI Card.

Take the MCI Card along on this trip and start earning miles for the next one. You'll earn frequent flyer miles on all your calls and save with the low rates you've come to expect from MCI. Before you know it, you'll be on your way to some other international destination.

Sign up for MCI by calling 1-800-FLY-FREE

Earn Frequent Flyer Miles.

Is this a great time, or what? :-)

Easy To Call Home.

1. To use your MCI Card, just dial the WorldPhone access number of the country you're calling from.
2. Dial or give the operator your MCI Card number.
3. Dial or give the number you're calling.

American Samoa	633-2MCI (633-2624)
# Antigua	1-800-888-8000
(Available from public card phones only)	#2
# Argentina (CC)	0-800-5-1002
# Aruba ÷	800-888-8
# Bahamas	1-800-888-8000
# Barbados	1-800-888-8000
# Belize	557 from hotels
	815 from pay phones
# Bermuda ÷	1-800-888-8000
# Bolivia ◆ (CC)	0-800-2222
# Brazil (CC)	000-8012
# British Virgin Islands ÷	1-800-888-8000
# Cayman Islands	1-800-888-8000
# Chile (CC)	
To call using CTC ■	800-207-300
To call using ENTEL ■	800-360-180
# Colombia (CC) ◆	980-16-0001
Collect Access in Spanish	980-16-1000
# Costa Rica ◆	0800-012-2222
# Dominica	1-800-888-8000
# Dominican Republic (CC) ÷	1-800-888-8000
Collect Access in Spanish	1121
# Ecuador (CC) ÷	999-170
El Salvador	800-1767
# Grenada ÷	1-800-888-8000
Guatemala (CC) ◆	9999-189
Guyana	177
# Haiti ÷ Collect Access	193
Collect Access in French/Creole	190
Honduras ÷	8000-122
# Jamaica ÷ Collect Access	1-800-888-8000
(From Special Hotels only)	873
From payphones	÷2
# Mexico (CC)	
Avantel	01-800-021-8000
Telmex ▲	001-800-674-7000
Mexico Access in Spanish	01-800-021-1000
# Netherlands Antilles (CC) ÷	001-800-888-8000
Nicaragua (CC)	166
(Outside of Managua, dial 02 first)	
Collect Access in Spanish from any public payphone	÷2
# Panama	108
Military Bases	2810-108
# Paraguay ÷	00-812-800
# Peru	0-800-500-10
# Puerto Rico (CC)	1-800-888-8000
# St. Lucia ÷	1-800-888-8000
# Trinidad & Tobago ÷	1-800-888-8000
# Turks & Caicos ÷	1-800-888-8000
# Uruguay	000-412
# U.S. Virgin Islands (CC)	1-800-888-8000
# Venezuela (CC) ÷ ◆	800-1114-0

Automation available from most locations. (CC) Country-to-country calling available to/from most international locations. ÷ Limited availability. ◆ Public phones may require deposit of coin or phone card for dial tone. ■ International communications carrier. ▲ When calling from public phones, use phones marked LADATEL. Limit one bonus program per MCI account. Terms and conditions apply. All airline program rules and conditions apply. ©1998 MCI Telecommunications Corporation. All rights reserved. Is this a great time, or what? is a service mark of MCI.

With guidebooks for every kind of travel—from weekend getaways to island hopping to adventures abroad—it's easy to understand why smart travelers go with **Fodor's**.

At bookstores everywhere.
www.fodors.com

Smart travelers go with **Fodor's** ™

KINGSTON

The most popular spots in Kingston are **Asylum** (⊠ 69 Knutsford Blvd., ☎ 876/929–5459), **Jonkanoo** (⊠ Wyndham New Kingston, 75 Knutsford Blvd., ☎ 876/929–3390), and the trendy disco **Mirage** (⊠ Sovereign Centre, ☎ 876/978–8557).

MONTEGO BAY

The hottest places in MoBay are **Walter's** (⊠ 39 Gloucester Ave., ☎ 876/952–9391), **Hurricanes Disco** (⊠ Breezes Montego Bay Resort, Gloucester Ave., ☎ 876/940–1150), and the **Rhythm Nightclub** (⊠ Holiday Inn Sunspree Resort, 6 mi east of airport on North Coast Hwy., ☎ 876/953–2485). After 10 on Friday nights, the crowd gathers at **Pier 1** (⊠ Howard Cooke Blvd., ☎ 876/952–2452) opposite the straw market. Two very popular new sports bars, both on Gloucester Avenue, are the **Brewery** (☎ 876/940–2433) and **Margueritaville** (☎ 876/952–4777).

NEGRIL

In Negril, you'll find the best music at **Alfred's Ocean Palace** (⊠ Norman Manley Blvd., ☎ 876/957–4735); **De Buss** (⊠ Norman Manley Blvd., ☎ 876/957–4405); the disco at **Hedonism II** (⊠ Norman Manley Blvd., ☎ 876/957–4200); and at the hot, hot spot **Kaiser's Cafe** (⊠ Lighthouse Rd., ☎ 876/957–4070).

OCHO RIOS

The principal clubs in Ocho Rios are **Acropolis** (⊠ 70 Main St., ☎ 876/974–2633); **Jamaic'N Me Crazy** (⊠ Renaissance Jamaica Grande, Main St., ☎ 876/974–2201); **Silks** (⊠ Shaw Park Beach Hotel, Shaw Park Ridge Rd., 1½ mi south of Ocho Rios, ☎ 876/974–2552); and the **Little Pub** (⊠ Main St., ☎ 876/974–2324), which produces Caribbean revues several nights a week.

PORT ANTONIO

In Port Antonio, if you have but one night to dance, do it at the **Roof Club** (⊠ 11 West St., ☎ 876/993–3817). On weekends, from 11 on, this is where it's all happening. An alternative for Port Antonio nightlife is the dance scene at **Shadows** (⊠ 40 West St., ☎ 876/993–3823) or the live jazz performances on Saturday evenings at the **Blue Lagoon Restaurant** (⊠ San San Beach, ☎ 876/993–8491).

7 Exploring Jamaica

TOURING JAMAICA CAN BE both thrilling and frustrating. Rugged (albeit beautiful) terrain and winding—often potholed—roads make for slow going. (In the rainy season from June through October, roads can be entirely washed out; *always* check conditions prior to heading out.) Primary roads that loop around and across the island are two lanes, signs are not prevalent, numbered addresses are seldom used outside of major townships, locals drive aggressively, and people and animals seem to have a knack for appearing out of nowhere before your vehicle. That said, Jamaica's scenery should not be missed. The solution? Stick to guided tours and licensed taxis—to be safe and to avoid frustration.

If you're staying in Kingston or Port Antonio, set aside at least one day for the capital city's highlights and another for a guided excursion to the Blue Mountains. If you have more time, head for Mandeville. You'll find at least three days' worth of activity right along MoBay's boundaries; you should also consider a trip to Cockpit Country or Ocho Rios. If you're based in Ocho Rios, be sure to visit Dunns' River Falls; you may also want to stop by Firefly or Port Antonio. If Negril is your hub, take in the south shore, including Y. S. Falls and the Black River.

Numbers in the margin correspond to points of interest on the Exploring Jamaica map.

Sights to See

❾ Blue Mountains. These lush mountains rise to the north of Kingston. If you admire Jamaica's coffee, be sure to visit **Pine Grove,** a working coffee farm that doubles as an inn. It also has a restaurant that serves owner Marcia Thwaites's Jamaican cuisine. Another place worth a visit is **Mavis Bank** and its Jablum coffee plant. This spot is surprisingly (and delightfully) primitive considering the retail price of the beans it processes. A half-hour guided tour is available for $5; inquire when you arrive at the main office. Stop in World's End for a free tour of **Dr. Sangster's Rum Factory** (☎ 876/926–8888; call ahead for tour reservations), open weekdays 8:30–4:30. The small factory produces wonderful liqueurs flavored with local coffee beans, oranges, coconuts, and other Jamaican produce; samples are part of the tour.

Unless you're traveling with a local, don't rent a car and go to the Blue Mountains on your own; the roads wind and dip, hand-lettered signs blow away, and you could easily get lost—not just for hours, but for days. It's best to hire a taxi (look for red PPV license plates to identify a licensed taxi) or to take a guided tour. Another way to see the Blue Mountains is on a downhill bicycle tour offered by **Blue Mountain Tours** (☞ Guided Tours, *below*).

⓮ Cockpit Country. Fifteen miles inland from MoBay is one of the most primitive areas in the West Indies: a terrain of pitfalls and potholes carved by nature in limestone. For nearly a century after 1655, it was known as the Land of Look Behind because British soldiers nervously rode their horses through here, always looking out for the savage freedom fighters known as Maroons. Fugitive slaves who refused to surrender to the invading English, the Maroons eventually won their independence. Today their descendents continue to live in this area, untaxed and virtually ungoverned by outside authorities. Most visitors stop in Accompong, a small community in St. Elizabeth Parish where you can stroll through town, take in a couple of historic structures, and learn more about the Maroons—considered Jamaica's greatest herbalists.

❺ Crystal Springs. About 18 mi west of Port Antonio on a former sugarcane plantation, Crystal Springs has more than 15,000 orchid blooms. The hummingbirds that dart among the blossoms here will land on your outstretched hand. Hiking and camping are options here; to camp, be sure to call the Jamaica Tourist Board (☞ Visitor Information *in* Essential Information) to arrange a site. ⊠ *Buff Bay,* ☎ *876/ 993–2609 or 876/996–1400.* ▱ *J$100.* ☼ *Daily 9–5.*

❹ Firefly. About 20 mi east of Ocho Rios in Port Maria, Firefly was once Sir Noël Coward's vacation home and is now maintained by the Jamaican National Heritage Trust. Although the setting is Eden-like, the house is surprisingly spartan, considering that he often entertained jet-setters and royalty. He wrote *High Spirits, Quadrille,* and other plays here, and his simple grave is on the grounds next to a small stage where his works are occasionally performed. Recordings of Coward singing about mad dogs and Englishmen echo over the lawns. Tours include time in the photo gallery and a walk through the house and grounds, the viewing of a video on Coward, and a drink in the gift shop. ✉ *Port Maria,* ☎ *876/997–7201.* 🎟 *$10.* ☉ *Daily 8:30–5:30.*

🔟 **Kingston.** The reaction of most newcomers to the capital is far from love at first sight. Yet the islanders themselves can't seem to let the city go. Everybody talks about it, about their homes or relatives there, about their childhood memories. Indeed, Kingston seems to reflect more of the true Jamaica—a wonderful cultural mix—than do the sunny havens of the north coast. As one Jamaican put it, "You don't really know Jamaica until you know Kingston." Parts of the city may be dirty, crowded, and raucous, yet it's still where international and local movers and shakers come to move and shake, where the arts flourish, and where the shopping is superb. It's also home to the University of the West Indies, which has departments devoted to Caribbean art and literature as well as to science.

Sprawling Kingston spills over into communities in every direction. To the west, coming in from Spanish Town, lie some of the city's worst slums in the neighborhoods of Six Miles and Riverton City. South along the waterfront, Spanish Town Road skirts through the downtown, a high-crime district that many Kingstonians avoid. In the heart of downtown, the pace is more peaceful, with a lovely waterfront walk and parks on Ocean Boulevard, near the world-class Jamaica Convention Centre, the home of the UN body that creates all laws for the world's seas. From the waterfront, you can look across Kingston Harbour to the Palisadoes Peninsula. This narrow strip is home to Norman Manley International Airport and, farther west, Port Royal, the island's former capital, which was destroyed by an earthquake. (A few words of caution: Downtown Kingston is considered unsafe, particularly at night, when even true Kingstonians beat a quick path out.)

New Kingston, north of downtown is bordered by Old Hope Road on the east and Half Way Tree Road (which changes to Constant Spring Road) on the west. The area is sliced

Exploring Jamaica

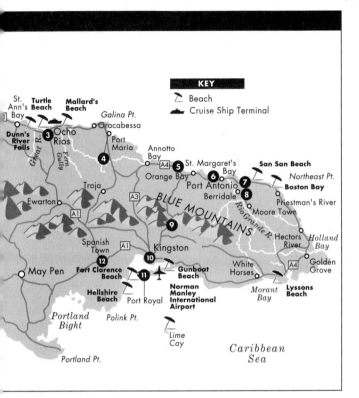

KEY

↗ Beach

⛴ Cruise Ship Terminal

St. Ann's Bay

Turtle Beach

Mallard's Beach

Galina Pt.

Dunn's River Falls

Ocho Rios

❸

Oracabessa

Port Maria

Annotto Bay

❹

Orange Bay

St. Margaret's Bay

San San Beach

Northeast Pt.

A4 **❺**

❻

Port Antonio

❼

Berridale

❽

Boston Bay

Priestman's River

Moore Town

Troja

Ewarton

A1

A3

BLUE MOUNTAINS

Rio Grande R.

Hectors River

Holland Bay

❾

Spanish Town

A1

Kingston

❿

Rio Grande R.

White Horses

A4

Golden Grove

May Pen

⓬

Fort Clarence Beach

⓫

Gunboat Beach

Morant Bay

Lyssons Beach

Hellshire Beach

Port Royal

Norman Manley International Airport

Portland Bight

Polink Pt.

Lime Cay

Caribbean Sea

Portland Pt.

by Hope Road, a major thoroughfare that connects this region with the University of the West Indies, about 15 minutes east of New Kingston. You may feel the most
comfortable in New Kingston, which glistens with hotels,
office towers, apartments, and boutiques. But don't let
your trip to the capital end here, though; away from the
high-rises of the new city, Kingston's colonial past is very
much alive.

North of New Kingston, the city gives way to steep hills
and magnificent homes. East of here, the views are even
grander as the road winds into the Blue Mountains. Hope
Road, just after the University of the West Indies, becomes
Gordon Town Road and starts twisting up through the
mountains—it's a route that leaves no room for error.

Devon House, built in 1881 and bought and restored by
the government in the 1960s, is filled with period furnishings, such as Venetian crystal chandeliers, and period reproductions. You can see the inside of the two-story mansion
(built with a South American gold miner's fortune) only on
a guided tour. On the grounds you'll find some of the best
crafts shops on the island (☞ Chapter 5) as well as one of
the few mahogany trees to have survived Kingston's ambitious, but not always careful, development. ⊠ *26 Hope
Rd.,* ☎ *876/929–7029.* ☎ *J$110 for house tour.* ☉ *Devon
House Tues.–Sat. 9:30–5, shops Mon.–Sat. 10–6.*

The **Institute of Jamaica,** near the waterfront, is a natural
history museum and library that traces the island's history
from the Arawaks through to current events. The charts
and almanacs here are often fascinating; the famed Shark
Papers, for example, contain evidence of wrongdoing by
a sea captain. (In an attempt to destroy this evidence, the
guilty captain tossed it overboard his ship, but it was later
recovered from the belly of a shark.) ⊠ *12 East St.,* ☎ *876/
922–0620.* ☎ *Museum $2, library free.* ☉ *Mon.–Thurs.
9–5, Fri. 9–4.*

The artists represented at the **National Gallery** may not be
household names in other nations, yet their paintings reveal a sensitivity that transcends academic training. You'll
find works by such intuitive Jamaican masters as John
Dunkley, David Miller Sr., and David Miller Jr. Among other

highlights from the 1920s through the 1980s are works by intuitive artist Kapo. Reggae fans should look for Christopher Gonzalez's controversial statue of Bob Marley. ⊠ *12 Ocean Blvd. (Kingston Mall, near the waterfront),* ☎ *876/ 922–1561.* 🎫 *J$40.* ⊘ *Weekdays 11–4:30.*

At the height of his career, Bob Marley built a recording studio. Today this structure—which is painted in Rastafarian red, yellow, and green—houses the **Bob Marley Museum**. The guided tour takes you through the medicinal herb garden and to the room where Marley was shot, his bedroom, and other rooms wallpapered with magazine and newspaper articles that chronicle his rise to stardom. The tour includes a 20-minute biographical film on him; there's also a reference library if you want to learn more. Certainly there's much here that will help you to understand Marley, reggae, and Jamaica itself. The Ethiopian flag is a reminder that Rastas consider the late Ethiopian emperor Haile Selassie, a descendant of King Solomon and the Queen of Sheba, to be the Messiah. A striking mural by Jah Bobby, *The Journey of Superstar Bob Marley,* depicts the hero's life from its beginnings in a womb shaped like a coconut to enshrinement in the hearts of the Jamaican people. ⊠ *56 Hope Rd.,* ☎ *876/927–9152.* 🎫 *J$350.* ⊘ *Mon.– Tues. and Thurs.–Fri. 9–5, Wed. and Sat. 12:30–6.*

Although no longer lovingly cared for, the **Royal Botanical Gardens at Hope** is a nice place to picnic or while away an afternoon. Donated to Jamaica by the Hope family following the abolition of slavery, the garden consists of 50 acres filled with tropical trees, plants, and flowers; most are clearly labeled. Free concerts are given here on the first Sunday of each month. ⊠ *Off Hope Rd.,* ☎ *876/927–1085.* 🎫 *J$20.* ⊘ *Weekdays 10–5, weekends 10–5:30.*

The **Rockfort Mineral Baths** are named for the stone fort that the British built above Kingston Harbour in 1694 and for the natural mineral spring that emerged after the devastating earthquake in 1907. Today, you can join the Kingstonians who come here to cool off in the public swimming pool that's filled with invigorating spring water or to unwind tense muscles in a private whirlpool tub. You can also visit the juice bar or the cafeteria before staking out a people-watching spot on the landscaped grounds. Baths must be booked in advance. ✉ *On A–1, just east of town,* ☎ *876/938–5055.* 🎫 *Pool J$70, private baths start at J$450.* ⏲ *Weekdays 6:30–6, weekends 8–6.*

13 **Mandeville.** At 2,000 ft above sea level, Mandeville is considerably cooler than the coastal areas 25 mi to the south. Its vegetation is also more lush, thanks to the mists that drift through the mountains. But climate and flora are not all that separates it from the steamy coast: Mandeville seems a hilly tribute to all that is genteel and admirable in the British character. The people here live their lives in tidy cottages with gardens around a village green; there's even a Georgian courthouse and a parish church. The entire scene could be set down in Devonshire, were it not for the occasional poinciana blossom or citrus grove.

The **Manchester Club** (☎ 876/962–2403) has tennis courts and a well-manicured 9-hole golf course, the first golf course in the Caribbean. Mrs. Stephenson conducts horticultural tours of her **gardens** (☎ 876/962–2328), which are filled with orchids and fruit trees. At the **Bird Sanctuary at Marshall's Penn Great House** (☎ 876/963–8569) you may spot some of the more than 25 species of birds indigenous to Jamaica. Tours (by appointment only) are led by owner Robert Sutton, one of the island's leading ornithologists. Other sights worth visiting are **Lover's Leap,** where legend has it that two slave lovers chose to jump off the 1,700-ft-high cliff rather than be recaptured by their owner, and the **High Mountain Coffee Plantation** (☎ 876/963–4211) in nearby Williamsfield, where free tours (by appointment only) show how coffee beans are turned into one of America's favorite morning drinks.

2 **Martha Brae River.** The gentle waterway takes its name from an Arawak Indian who killed herself because she refused to reveal the whereabouts of a local gold mine to the Spanish. According to legend, she agreed to take them there and, on reaching the river, used magic to change its course, drowning herself and the greedy Spaniards. Her *duppy* (ghost) is said to guard the mine's entrance. Rafting on this river is a very popular activity, and **Martha Brae River Rafting** (☞ Guided Tours, *below*) arranges trips down river. The rafting company ticket office, gift shops, a bar-restaurant, and a swimming pool are at the top of the river.

❶ Montego Bay. Today many explorations of MoBay are conducted from a reclining chair—frothy drink in hand—on Doctor's Cave Beach. Believe it or not, the area had a history before all the resorts went up. If you can pull yourself away from the water's edge and brush the sand off your toes, you'll find some very interesting colonial sights.

The outstanding tour of **Barnett Estates** is led by a charming guide in period costume who recites period poetry and sings period songs. The Kerr-Jarrett family has held the land here for 11 generations, and they still grow coconut, mango, and sugarcane on 3,000 acres; you'll get samples during the optional plantation tour by horseback (one hour), which follows the tour of the great house. ⊠ *Granville Main Rd.,* ☎ *876/952–2382,* ☒ *876/952–6342.* 🎫 *Great house tour $10, great house and plantation tour $45.* ☉ *Great house 9:30 AM–10 PM; tours daily at 10 and 2.*

In the 1700s **Rose Hall** may well have been the greatest of great houses in the West Indies. Today it's popular less for its architecture than for the legend surrounding its second mistress: Annie Palmer was credited with murdering three husbands and a *busha* (plantation overseer) who was her lover. The story is told in a novel that's sold everywhere in Jamaica: *The White Witch of Rose Hall.* There's a pub on-site. ⊠ *East of Montego Bay, across highway from Rose Hall resorts,* ☎ *876/953–2323.* 🎫 *$15.* ☉ *Daily 9–6.*

Greenwood Great House has no spooky legend to titillate you, but it's much better than Rose Hall at evoking the atmosphere of life on a sugar plantation. The Barrett family, from which the English poet Elizabeth Barrett Browning descended, once owned all the land from Rose Hall to Falmouth and built this and several other great houses on it. (The poet's father, Edward Moulton Barrett, "the Tyrant of Wimpole Street," was born at Cinnamon Hill, currently the estate of country singer Johnny Cash.) Highlights of Greenwood include oil paintings of the Barretts, china made for the family by Wedgwood, a library filled with rare books printed as early as 1697, fine antique furniture, and a collection of exotic musical instruments. There's a pub on-site as well. ⊠ *15 mi east of Montego Bay,* ☎ *876/953–1077.* 🎫 *$10.* ☉ *Daily 9–6.*

⑮ Negril. In the 18th century, this was where English ships assembled in convoys for dangerous ocean crossings. The infamous pirate Calico Jack and his crew were captured right here, while they guzzled rum. All but two of them were hanged on the spot; Mary Read and Anne Bonney were pregnant at the time, so their executions were delayed.

On the winding coast road 55 mi southwest of MoBay, Negril was once Jamaica's best-kept secret. Recently, however, it has begun to shed some of its bohemian, ramshackle atmosphere for the attractions and activities traditionally associated with Montego Bay. Applauding the sunset from Rick's Cafe may still be a highlight in Negril, yet, increasingly, the hours before and after are filled with conventional recreation. One thing that hasn't changed around this west coast center (whose only true claim to fame is a 7-mi beach) is the casual approach to life. As you wander from lunch in the sun to shopping in the sun to sports in the sun, you'll find that swimsuits are common attire. Want to dress for a special meal? Slip a caftan over your swimsuit.

Negril stretches along the coast south from the horseshoe-shape **Bloody Bay** (named during the period when it was a whale-processing center) along the calm waters of **Long Bay** to the Lighthouse (☞ *below*) section and the landmark **Rick's Cafe** (☞ Chapter 3). Sunset at Rick's is a Negril tradition. Divers spiral downward off 50-ft-high cliffs into the deep green depths as the sun turns into a ball of fire and sets the clouds ablaze with color.

Even nonguests can romp at **Hedonism II** (☞ Chapter 2) for a day. The resort beach is divided into a "prude" and "nude" side but a quick look around the property reveals where most guests pull their chaise longue. Volleyball, body-painting contests, and shuffleboard—all done in the nude—keep daytime hours lively; at night most action occurs in the high-tech disco or in the nude hot tub. Your day (10:30–5) pass ($50) gets you a taste of the spirit as well as the food and drink—and participation in water sports, tennis, squash, and other activities. Night passes ($35) cover dinner, drinks, and entrance to the disco. Day or night, reservations are a must.

The **Anancy Family Fun & Nature Park** (✉ Norman Manley Blvd., ☎ 876/957–5100) is named after a mischievous spider character in Jamaican folktales. The 3-acre site has an 18-hole miniature golf course, go-cart rides, a minitrain, a fishing pond, a nature trail, and three small museums— one dedicated to crafts, another to conservation, and the third to heritage.

Around sunset **Norman Manley Boulevard,** which intersects with **West End Road,** Negril's main (and only) thoroughfare, comes to life with bustling bistros and ear-splitting discos. West End Road leads to the town's only building of historical significance, the **Lighthouse.** You can stop by the adjacent caretaker's cottage and, for the price of a tip, climb the spiral steps to the best view in town.

❸ **Ocho Rios.** Although Ocho Rios is not near eight rivers as its name implies, it does have a seemingly endless series of cascades that sparkle from limestone rocks along the coast. (The name Ocho Rios came about because the English misunderstood the Spanish name "Las Chorreras" or "the waterfalls.")

For as long as anyone can remember, Ocho Rios has been the Jamaicans' favorite escape from the heat of Kingston. Indeed, they can fill the place by themselves, especially on a busy market day, when cars and buses from the countryside clog the coastal road that links Port Antonio with Montego Bay. Add a tour bus or three and the entire passenger list from a cruise ship, and you may find yourself mired in a major traffic jam.

Yet a visit to Ocho Rios is worthwhile, if only to enjoy its two chief attractions—Dunn's River Falls and Prospect Plantation. A few steps from the main road in Ocho Rios are some of the most charming inns and oceanfront restaurants in the Caribbean. Lying on the sand of what seems to be your very own cove or swinging gently in a hammock while sipping a tropical drink, you'll soon forget the traffic that's just a stroll away.

Dunn's River Falls is an eye-catching sight: 600 ft of cold, clear mountain water splashing over a series of stone steps to the warm Caribbean. The best way to enjoy the falls is to climb the slippery steps: don a swimsuit, take the hand of the person ahead of you, and trust that the chain of hands and bodies leads to an experienced guide. The leaders of the climbs are personable fellows who reel off bits of local lore while telling you where to step. ⊠ *Off A–1, between St. Ann's and Ocho Rios,* ☎ *876/974–2857.* 🎫 *$6.* ☉ *Daily 8:30–4.*

To learn about Jamaica's former agricultural lifestyle, a trip to **Prospect Plantation** is a must. But it's not just a place for history lovers or farming aficionados; everyone seems to enjoy the views over the White River Gorge and the tour by jitney (a canopied open-air cart pulled by a tractor). The grounds are full of exotic fruits and tropical trees, some planted over the years by such celebrities as Winston Churchill and Charlie Chaplin. You can also go horseback riding on the plantation's 900 acres or play miniature golf, grab a drink in the bar, or buy souvenirs in the gift shop. If you want more time to really explore, you can rent one of the on-site villas. ⊠ *Hwy. A–1, just west of downtown Ocho Rios,* ☎ *876/994–1058.* 🎫 *$12.* ☉ *Daily 8–5. Tours Mon.–Sat. at 10:30, 2, and 3:30; Sun. at 11, 1:30, and 3:30.*

The original "defenders" stationed at the **Old Fort,** which was built in 1777, spent much of their time sacking and plundering as far afield as St. Augustine, Florida, and sharing their bounty with the local plantation owners who financed their missions. Fifteen miles west is **Discovery Bay,** site of Columbus's landing, with a small museum of artifacts and Jamaican memorabilia.

Jamaica's national motto is "Out of Many, One People," and at the **Coyaba River Garden and Museum** you can see exhibits on the many cultural influences that have contributed to the creation of the one. The museum covers the island's history from the time of the Arawak Indians up to the modern day. A guided 45-minute tour through the lush 3-acre garden introduces you to the flora and fauna of the island. The complex includes a crafts and gift shop and a snack bar. ⊠ *Shaw Park Estate, Shaw Park Ridge Rd., 1½ mi south of Ocho Rios,* ☎ *876/974–6235.* 🎫 *$4.50.* ☉ *Daily 8–5.*

Other excursions of note include Runaway Bay's **Green Grotto Caves** (and the boat ride on an underground lake); a ramble through the **Shaw Park Botanical Gardens**; a visit to **Sun Valley**, a working plantation with banana, coconut, and citrus trees; and a drive through **Fern Gully**, a natural canopy of vegetation filtered by sunlight (Jamaica has the world's largest number of fern species, more than 570).

⑦ Port Antonio. Early in the century the first tourists who arrived on the northeast coast were drawn by the exoticism of the island's banana trade and seeking a respite from the New York winters. The original posters of the shipping lines make Port Antonio appear as foreign as the moon, yet in time it became the tropical darling of a fast-moving crowd and counted J. P. Morgan, Rudyard Kipling, William Randolph Hearst, Clara Bow, Bette Davis, and Ginger Rogers among its admirers. Its most passionate devotee was the actor Errol Flynn, whose spirit still seems to haunt the docks, devouring raw dolphinfish and swigging gin at 10 AM. Although the action has moved elsewhere, the area can still weave a spell. Robin Moore wrote *The French Connection* here, and Broadway's tall and talented Tommy Tune found inspiration for the musical *Nine* while being pampered at Trident.

Port Antonio has also long been a center for some of the Caribbean's finest deep-sea fishing. Dolphins (the delectable fish, not the lovable mammal) are the likely catch here, along with tuna, kingfish, and wahoo. In October the weeklong Blue Marlin Tournament attracts anglers from around the world. By the time everyone has had their fill of beer, it's the fish stories—rather than the fish—that carry the day.

The town's best-known landmark is **Folly**, a Roman-style villa in ruins on the eastern edge of East Harbor. The creation of a Connecticut millionaire in 1905, the manse was made almost entirely of concrete. Unfortunately, the cement was mixed with seawater, and it began to crumble as it dried. According to local lore, the millionaire's bride took one look at her shattered dream, burst into tears, and fled forever. Little more than the marble floor remains today. (Note that Folly becomes something of a ganja—marijuana—hangout after sundown and should be avoided then.)

A good way to spend a day in Port Antonio is swimming in the deep azure water of the **Blue Lagoon**. Although there's not much beach to speak of, you will find a water-sports center, changing rooms, and a soothing mineral pool. Yummy, inexpensive, Jamaican fare is served at a charming waterside terrace restaurant; it's open daily for lunch and dinner and has live jazz music on Saturday night. ⊠ *1 mi east of San San Beach,* ☎ *876/993–8491.*

Queen Street, in the residential Titchfield area, a couple of miles north of downtown Port Antonio, has several fine examples of Georgian architecture. **DeMontevin Lodge** (⊠ 21 Fort George St., on Titchfield Hill, ☎ 876/993–2604), owned by the Mullings family (the late Gladys Mullings was Errol Flynn's cook, and you can still get great food here), and structures on the nearby **Musgrave Street** (the crafts market is here) are in a traditional seaside style that's reminiscent of architecture found in New England.

A short drive east from Port Antonio puts you at **Boston Bay,** which is popular with swimmers and has been enshrined by lovers of jerk pork. The spicy barbecue was originated by the Arawaks and perfected by runaway slaves called the Maroons. Eating almost nothing but wild hog preserved over smoking coals enabled them to survive years of fierce guerrilla warfare with the English.

Some 6 mi northeast of Port Antonio in the village of Nonsuch are the **Athenry Gardens**, a 3-acre tropical wonderland, and the **Nonsuch Caves**, whose underground beauty has been made accessible by concrete walkways, railed stairways, and careful lighting. ⊠ *Athenry/Nonsuch, first right after Dragon Bay east of Port Antonio,* ☎ *876/993– 3740.* ▨ *$5.* ☺ *Daily 10–4:30.*

⑪ **Port Royal.** Just south of Kingston, Port Royal was called "the wickedest city in the world"—before an earthquake tumbled it into the sea in 1692. The spirits of Henry Morgan and other buccaneers add a great deal of energy to what remains. The proudest possession of St. Peter's Church, rebuilt in 1726 to replace Christ's Church, is a silver communion set said to have been donated by Morgan himself (who probably obtained it during a raid on Panama).

Port Royal is slated for a massive redevelopment project that will renovate existing historical sites and introduce new museums, shops, restaurants, and perhaps even a cruise-ship pier. However, funding for these ambitious plans was not yet in place at press time.

A ferry from the square in downtown Kingston goes to Port Royal at least twice a day, and the town is small enough to see on foot. If you drive out to Port Royal from Kingston, you'll pass several other sights, including remains of old forts virtually covered over by vegetation, an old naval cemetery (which has some intriguing headstones), and a monument commemorating Jamaica's first coconut tree, planted in 1863 (there's no tree there now, just plenty of cactus and scrub brush).

You can no longer down rum in Port Royal's legendary 40 taverns (well, two small pubs still remain in operation), but you can explore the impressive remains of **Ft. Charles**, once the area's major garrison. Built in 1662, this is the oldest surviving monument of the British occupation of Jamaica. On the grounds is a maritime museum and the old artillery storehouse, Giddy House, that gained its name after being tilted by the earthquake of 1907 (locals say its slant makes you giddy). In the graveyard of **St. Peter Church** is the tombstone of Lewis Galdy, who was swallowed up in the 1692 quake, spewed into the sea, rescued, and lived another two decades in "Great Reputation." Nearby is the tomb of three small children, victims of the earthquake, whose bodies were recovered by archaeologists from Texas A&M University. ☎ *876/967–8059 (church).* 🎫 *$4.* ☉ *Daily 9–5.*

❽ Rio Grande River. The Rio Grande (yes, Jamaica has a Rio Grande, too) is a granddaddy of river-rafting attractions: an 8-mi-long, swift, green waterway from Berrydale to Rafter's Rest (it flows into the Caribbean at St. Margaret's Bay). The trip of about three hours is made on bamboo rafts pushed along by a raftsman who is likely to be a character. You can pack a picnic lunch and eat it on the raft or along the riverbank; wherever you lunch, a vendor of Red Stripe beer will appear at your elbow. A restaurant, bar, and souvenir shops are at Rafter's Rest. The trip costs about $40 per two-person raft (☞ Guided Tours, *below*).

❻ Somerset Falls. At this sun-dappled spot crawling with flowering vines, you can climb the 400-ft falls with some assistance from a concrete staircase. A brief raft ride takes you part of the way. ⊠ *North Coast Hwy.* 🎫 *J$35.* ☉ *Daily 10–5.*

⓬ Spanish Town. Twelve miles west of Kingston on A–1, Spanish Town was the island's capital under Spanish rule. The town has the tiered Georgian **Antique Square,** the Jamaican People's Museum of Crafts and Technology (in the Old King's House stables), and **St. James,** the oldest cathedral in the Western Hemisphere. Spanish Town's original name was Santiago de la Vega, which the English corrupted to St. Jago de la Vega, meaning St. James of the Plains. Contact the Institute of Jamaica (☎ 876/922–0620) for further information on this heritage town.

Guided Tours

Half-day tours are offered by a variety of operators in the important areas of Jamaica. The best great-house tours include Rose Hall, Greenwood, and Devon House. Plantations to tour are Prospect, Barnett Estates, and Sun Valley. The Appleton Estate Tour uses a bus to visit villages, plantations, and a rum distillery. The increasingly popular waterside folklore feasts are offered on the Dunn's, Great, and White rivers. The significant city tours are in Kingston, Montego Bay, and Ocho Rios. Quality tour operators include **Caribic Tours** (⊠ 1310 Providence Dr., MoBay, ☎ 876/953–9895), **CS Tours** (⊠ 66 Claude Clarke Ave., MoBay, ☎ 876/952–6260), **Glamour Tours** (⊠ Montego Freeport, MoBay, ☎ 876/979–8415), **SunHoliday Tours** (⊠ 57 S. James St. or Sangster International Airport, MoBay, ☎ 876/952–5629), and **Tourwise** (⊠ 103 Main St., Ocho Rios, ☎ 876/974–2323).

Boat Trips

An Evening on the Great River (⊠ 4 Sewell Ave., ☎ 876/952–5047 or 876/952–5097) includes a boat ride up the torch-lit river, a full Jamaican dinner, an open bar, a folklore show, and dancing to a reggae band. It costs around $60 per person with hotel pickup and return, less if you arrive via your own transport. Tours are offered Sunday–

Thursday. **Calico Sailing** (⊠ North Coast Highway, ☎ 876/952–5860) offers snorkeling trips and sunset cruises on the waters of Montego Bay; costs are $35 and $25, respectively. **Martha Brae River Rafting** (⊠ Claude Clarke Ave., ☎ 876/952–0889) leads trips down the Martha Brae River, about 25 mi from most hotels in Montego Bay. The cost is just under $40 per raft (two per raft) for the 1½-hour river run. **Mountain Valley Rafting** (⊠ Lethe, ☎ 876/952–0527 or 876/952–6388) runs trips down the River Lethe, approximately 12 mi (about 50 minutes) southwest of Montego Bay. The hour-long trip is about $45 per raft (two per raft) and takes you through unspoiled hillside country. Bookings can also be made through hotel tour desks.

Rio Grande Attractions Ltd. (⊠ St. Margaret's Bay, ☎ 876/993–2778) guides raft trips down the Rio Grande (☞ Exploring, *above*). The cost is $40 per raft. **South Coast Safaris Ltd.** (⊠ 1 Crane Rd., Black River, ☎ 876/965–2513) has guided boat excursions up the Black River for some 10 mi (round-trip), into the mangroves and marshlands to see the alligators, birds, and plant life, aboard the 25-passenger *Safari Queen* and 25-passenger *Safari Princess*. The cost is around $15. **Undersea Tours MoBay** (⊠ Casa Blanca Hotel, Gloucester Ave., ☎ 876/922–1287) offers you a good look at MoBay's marine sanctuary without getting wet, by booking passage (around $40) on a semisubmersible craft.

Helicopter Views

Helitours Jamaica Ltd. (⊠ 1 mi west of Ocho Rios, North Coast Hwy., ☎ 876/974–2265 or 876/974–1108), in Ocho Rios, offers helicopter tours of Jamaica, ranging from 20 minutes to an hour at prices that vary accordingly ($65–$225).

Special-Interest Tours

Blue Mountain Tours (⊠ Shop 15, Santa Maria Plaza, Ocho Rios, ☎ 876/974–7705, FAX 876/974–0635) offers a day-long downhill bicycle tour of the mountains, which coasts 18 mi down from 5,060 ft through coffee plantations and rain forests. The cost is about $80 and includes lunch. **Countrystyle** (⊠ 62 Ward Ave., Mandeville, ☎ 876/962–3725 or 800/JAMAICA) offers unique, personalized tours of island communities. You're linked with community residents based on your interests; there are tours that include anything from bird-watching in Mandeville to nightlife in Kingston. **Maroon Attraction Tours Co.** (⊠ North Coast Hwy., ☎ 876/952–4546) leads full-day tours from Montego Bay to Maroon headquarters at Accompong, giving you a glimpse of the society of Maroons, descendants of fugitive slaves, who live in Cockpit Country. The cost is under $50 per person. **Touring Society of Jamaica** (☎ 876/975–7158 in Ocho Rios, 876/967–1792 in Kingston), operated by American Lynda Lee Burke, offers several eco-tours, from birding in the Blue Mountains to exploring the natural history of Cockpit Country.

8 Portrait of Jamaica

WHAT IS JERK?

JERK COOKING IS AN AUTHENTIC Jamaican way to cook pork, chicken, seafood, and beef over a fire pit or on a barbecue grill. But it is the special seasoning—a highly spiced combination of scallions, onions, thyme, Jamaican pimento (allspice), cinnamon, nutmeg, peppers, and salt—that makes jerk what it is. To me, jerk cooking is the perfect reflection of the Jamaican lifestyle—spicy, sweet, charismatic, and hot.

The taste of jerked foods is hot with peppers, but as you savor it, the variety of spices catches up with you, and it is like a carnival where all the elements come together in your mouth. The combination of spices tastes as if they were quarreling and dancing and mingling in your mouth all at the same time. It is not a predictable flavor, but rather a hot, spicy, uncontrolled festival that engages all your senses. It is so unexpected a taste that, in spite of its peppery heat, you automatically want more. We have a saying in Jamaica, "It is very morish"—you want more.

People always ask me, "How did jerk get its name?" I really don't know, but I can tell you almost everyone has a pet theory. Some people say it is called jerk because the meat is turned over and over again—or jerked over and over again—as it cooks over the fire. Others say that is not right; it is called jerk because, when it is served, the jerk man pulls—or, you see, jerks—a portion of meat off the pork. To me, it does not matter what is called, or why. What counts is flavor.

The spices that are used in jerk seasoning have a very special pungency. Jamaican spices are world famous—their oil content is said to be higher than anywhere else in the world, and it is the very oiliness of the spices that intensifies the zip and zest. (It is even said that in World War I, European soldiers were told to line their boots with Jamaican pimento as a way to make their feet warmer in the cold winters.)

Jerk huts are everywhere in Jamaica. You see them clustered by the side of the road, a medley of huts. There is always a wonderful

---

smoky aroma hovering over the huts—the pungency of the burning pimento woods and spices mingling with the delicious scent of the meat. And everywhere are buses, trucks, cars, and vans disgorging hungry passengers in search of jerk pork, jerk chicken, escovitch fish, salt fish and ackee, roast yam, roast plantain, boiled corn, rice and peas, cock soup, mannish water, Irish moss, and festival! Everything that the Jamaicans love is found at the jerk huts, embellished with a great deal of spice. And the cries from each hut: "Which jerk you want?" "Taste mine!"

JERK HUTS ARE USU-ALLY octagonal or circular, with a telephone pole in the center supporting a thatched or shingled roof. There is a seating bar around the outside of the hut. The food is jerked outside, either in a lean-to attached to the hut, or in a separate hut of its own, or even under a tree. There is rarely any such thing as a parking lot—you park on the side of the road, and you are greeted warmly by the proprietor and the amiable strangers there. You will also see the other customers who are impatiently waiting to sink their teeth into the delicious slabs of meat.

All jerk huts and shacks are very casual affairs, but if it is an especially rustic jerk hut, you can saunter over and pick out what you want directly from the fire. The jerk man or woman will then use a cleaver to slice off whatever you have requested and probably will weigh it to know what to charge you. The meat is served wrapped in foil or on a paper plate. Pork is usually cubed for you on the spot and you stand right there and eat it with your fingers. Chicken tends to be a bit juicier than pork so you really need several napkins to handle that. Usually the meat is very tender because it has been marinated for some time and then cooked slowly. In addition to the pork and chicken, you can get some jerk sausage, and even jerked lobster if you are up on the northern coast of the island.

You must always eat jerk with something sweet or bland to cut the heat—either some festival, a little like a sweet hush puppy, or some hard dough bread, a soft, flat bagel-type bread. Of course, you must cool the mouth with Jamaican Red Stripe beer, Ting great-fruit soda, or a rum concoction. And there is usually music, music, music.

If you are in Jamaica, the best place to look for jerk is in Boston, near Boston Beach, the home of the original jerk pits. The Pork Pit in Montego Bay next to the Casa Montego Hotel (3½ miles from the Montego Bay Airport) and the Ocho Rios Jerk Center (6

Main Street, Ocho Rios) are also famous jerk pits. In Negril, jerk pits line the two main roads that lead in and out of town; in Port Antonio, look for jerk on West Street, near the market.

JERKING PORK HAS BEEN in Jamaica a long time, at least since the middle of the seventeenth century. The method of pit-cooking meat was brought to the island by African hunters who had been enslaved by the British. Quite possibly these West African hunters adapted the seasoning methods of the native Arawak Indians, especially in their use of chile peppers. But it was not until the middle of the eighteenth century, during the guerilla wars between the escaped ex-slaves, known as Maroons, and England, that there was any real record of this method of preserving pork.

To the Maroon guerilla bands, the little wild boars that darted through the bush were a wonderful source of food. While some men kept watch on movements of the Redcoats on the plains, others, equipped with long spears, undertook the equally arduous task of pursuing the slippery animals to their lairs in almost inaccessible parts of the mountains.

But caught and killed at last, the boars were brought down from the mountaintops on long sticks to provide food for the weary rebels. Although some meat was eaten at the time of the hunt, most had to be preserved until the next opportunity to hunt presented itself—and who could tell when that would be?

The jerk seasoning combination, laced heavily with salt and peppers, was a means of preservation. The pork was slathered with the aromatic spice combination and wrapped in leaves. Some buried the wrapped marinated pig in a hole in the ground filled with hot stones, and the pork would steam slowly in its own juices. Others would grill it slowly—oh, so slowly, for 12 or 14 hours—over a fire of green wood. This was jerk cooking.

A peace treaty was finally signed by the opposing forces, but jerking pork was now deep in the Jamaican psyche.

Nowadays, it is common to barbeque pork over pimento wood to give the flesh that tangy flavor inherent in the pimento tree; but it was not always so. Those early Maroons used not only the wood of another tree, but also a number of strange herbs to season the meat. The practice was always secret and, even today, if one asked the descendant of a Maroon where his wood and those herbs could be found, he would wave his hand vaguely to the surrounding hills, and say, "Over there."

This wonderful secret way to prepare meat became part of the Jamaican life-style only about 15 years ago. Now there are jerk huts everywhere—in every town, every village, in every city in Jamaica.

Jerking is the latest food craze sweeping the island. It is no longer confined to pork, but now includes fish and chicken. Although jerk pork originally led the field, jerk chicken is now most popular. In Kingston, the capital of Jamaica, the demand for jerk chicken on the weekends is incredible. The steel drums converted to grills are now ubiquitous. They line the streets and, on a weekend in certain sections of Red Hills Road, so much smoke emerges from the line of drums that, except for the smell, one could be forgiven for thinking that a San Franciscan fog had come to Jamaica.

To eat jerk is to feel the influences from which it developed. It is as if you can hear the African, Indian, and calypso cultures that produced it. Jamaicans are great harmonizers—we make delicious soups, we keep our friends forever, we are fantastic musicians and artists—and we have applied this same harmony to our jerk seasoning.

— Helen Willinsky

INDEX

X = *restaurant*, 🏨 = *hotel*

WHEREVER YOU TRAVEL, *H*ELP IS NEVER FAR AWAY.

From planning your trip to providing travel assistance along the way, American Express® Travel Service Offices are always there to help you do more.

Jamaica

KINGSTON
Grace Kennedy Travel Ltd.
19-21 Knutsford Boulevard
876/929-6290

MONTEGO BAY
Allied Insurance Brokers
2 Market Street
876/952-9470

Travel
www.americanexpress.com/travel

American Express Travel Service Offices are located throughout Jamaica.